ZICK RUBIN is Louis an[...]chology at Brandeis Unive[...]e was born in 1944 and hold[...]e University of Michigan. [...]l *Sociometry*, General Editor[...]*al Behavior* series, and the author of numerous books, articles and papers in the field of social psychology.

The Editors of *The Developing Child*

JEROME BRUNER helped found the Center for Cognitive Studies at Harvard in 1960, and served there as Director until 1972. He is currently Watts Professor of Psychology at the University of Oxford and Fellow of Wolfson College, Oxford. He has long been interested in the nature of perception, thought, learning, and language, and has published widely on these topics. At present he is focusing his research on the early development of language in infants and on the role of the pre-school in early child development.

MICHAEL COLE is a professor in the Department of Communications, University of California, San Diego. Trained initially as a psychologist, his research in recent years has led him into the fields of anthropology and linguistics in an attempt to understand better the influence of different cultural institutions, especially formal schooling, on the development of children. He is the editor of *Soviet Psychology*, and his most recent book, co-authored with Sylvia Scribner, is entitled *Culture and Thought*.

BARBARA LLOYD is Reader in Social Psychology at the University of Sussex, author of *Perception and Cognition: a Cross-Cultural Perspective*, and editor (with John Archer) of *Exploring Sex Differences*. Her interest in child development has always been strongly cross-cultural (her first research was published as part of the Whitings' *Six Cultures* study). She has recently investigated cognitive development among both English and Nigerian children.

THE DEVELOPING CHILD edited by
Jerome Bruner, Michael Cole, Barbara Lloyd

PUBLISHED

FORTHCOMING

CHILDREN'S FRIENDSHIPS

Zick Rubin

FONTANA PAPERBACKS

To my mother
Adena Rubin

First published by Fontana Paperbacks 1980

Set in 'Monophoto' Plantin

Made and printed in Great Britain by
William Collins Sons & Co Ltd, Glasgow

Contents

Editors' Preface

Recent decades have witnessed unprecedented advances in research on human development. Each book in *The Developing Child* reflects the importance of this research as a resource for enhancing children's well-being. It is the purpose of the series to make this resource available to that increasingly large number of people who are responsible for raising a new generation. We hope that these books will provide rich and useful information for parents, educators, child-care professionals, students of developmental psychology and all others concerned with childhood.

JEROME BRUNER, *University of Oxford*
MICHAEL COLE, *University of California, San Diego*
BARBARA LLOYD, *University of Sussex*

Acknowledgements

Most of my career as a social psychologist has been devoted to the study of adult social behaviour. The shift to children's friendships was a new enterprise, one that I could not have carried out successfully without a great deal of help from others. The Foundation for Child Development, the National Institute of Mental Health, and the Social Science Research Council provided funds that enabled me to spend the year 1977–8 at the Institute of Human Development at the University of California, Berkeley, where I immersed myself in the social world of young children and began to write this book. At Berkeley I received invaluable assistance from many researchers, staff members, and nursery school teachers, including especially Paul Mussen, Jane Hunt, Hannah Sanders, Barbara Scales, and Louise Singleton.

In the preparation of this book I received continued financial assistance from the Foundation for Child Development, accompanied by the moral support of Orville G. Brim, Jr., and Heidi Sigal at the Foundation. I owe a special debt to Peggy Stubbs, who graciously made available to me the extensive logs about friendships that older children had written for her when she was their teacher. Among the many colleagues who have provided me with unpublished materials and have commented on portions of the manuscript, I am especially indebted to Gary Fine, Joseph Jacobson, Michael Lougee, and Elliot Medrich.

Once again, I am grateful to Carol Rubin, for her valuable comments on the manuscript, her encouragement, and her love.

Finally, I would like to express my thanks to the nursery school children at the Harold Jones Child Study Center in Berkeley and to Elihu Rubin and his friends in Berkeley and Boston, for letting me observe the development of their friendships.

1/Do Friends Matter?

Ricky and Danny are bright, alert three-year-olds who attend the same nursery class five mornings a week. Although Ricky did not enter the school until several weeks into the autumn term, he quickly proceeded to establish friendly relations with at least ten of the other children in the large class. He was successful from the outset in engaging others in activities of his own choosing. 'Come on, let's chase someone,' Ricky yells to one group of boys, and they follow in his tracks. He also joins in with other children's activities, praises them for their accomplishments, and shows concern for their welfare. 'Look what I made,' Sally says to Ricky. 'I put the cars together.' 'See, I told you you could do it,' Ricky replies. When Josh constructs an impressive building, Ricky tells him, 'That's really neat, Josh.' In return, Ricky receives the friendship and admiration of his classmates. He is by far the most popular boy in the class, and choruses of 'Ricky, will you play with us?' and 'Ricky had a good idea!' are commonly heard in the playground. 'It's good to have friends,' Ricky explains, ''cause I like friends – Josh, Tony, Caleb, David too. They're all my friends.'

Danny is just as eager as Ricky to have friends, but had a harder time of it. Early in the year he rarely approached other children and much of the time could be found wandering about the spacious playground by himself. He was most conspicuous during song time, when he would go into extended renditions of songs he had learned at home. As the term progressed, Danny made periodic attempts to join other children in their activities, but with little success. He approaches Alison and Becky, who are playing with puzzles, and stands beside them. 'Move,' Alison says. 'Why?' asks Danny. 'Because I don't want you here.' Danny goes off quietly. On another occasion Danny goes up to the table where Josh is working and says, 'Hi.' Josh doesn't reply, and Danny drifts away. Since he cannot seem to engage other children, Danny turns to the teachers. While several other children are playing with coloured plastic tubes, Danny takes some of the tubes and asks the head teacher, 'Will you do this with me, Mrs Benson?' When she suggests that he play with Dylan, Danny takes the pieces on his arm, sings a song to no one in particular, and goes off to a distant table by himself. Another time, Danny and Kevin are swinging from ropes together. Then Kevin runs off to the rocking boat, calling to his best friend Jake to join him. Danny is left to swing by himself. He walks slowly over to the schoolyard fence and looks through a crack to the adjacent schoolyard where unknown children from the other class are playing. When asked who his best friend in school is, Danny replies, 'Caleb.' When asked why, he answers forthrightly, 'I want him to be.'

Ricky and Danny have had very different experiences with friends and friendships during their first year in nursery school. It is clear that for both of them, however, friends matter a great deal. Not all three-year-olds or all older children are as concerned about friends as Ricky and Danny are. At varying points in development, some children may be more interested in painting or reading or even daydreaming than in interacting with other children. But, for the most part, friendships are among the central ingredients of children's lives, from as early as age three – or, in some cases, even earlier – through adolescence. Friendships occupy, both in their actual conduct and in the world of thought and fantasy, a large proportion of children's waking hours. They are often the sources of children's greatest pleasures and deepest frustrations.

In light of the importance of children's friendships, it is surprising to discover that social scientists have paid relatively little attention to them. Considerable research on young children's relations with one another was carried out in the 1920s and 1930s, but there was a prolonged period of neglect until a resurgence of research in the 1970s. One of the reasons for this neglect was the assumption, fostered by psychoanalytic theory, that the mother–child relationship is paramount in the child's development. Compared to this 'first relationship', children's relationships with one another were seen as being of little real importance. As a result, there was a tremendous outpouring of research on mother–child interaction, the effects of maternal (and sometimes paternal) deprivation, and disciplinary techniques, and almost no research at all on the relationships between children and their friends. Even those researchers who did focus on children's peer relations were likely to take the attitude that these relations were both overshadowed and determined by mother–child relations. Susan Isaacs, one of the best-known of these early researchers, concluded: 'In the earlier years, the child is very largely a naive egoist, and other children are to him mainly rivals for the love and approval of adults.'[1]

The lack of research on young children's friendships may also have reflected a social context in which preschool children were given relatively few opportunities to interact with their peers. More recently, such opportunities have greatly increased with the flourishing of playgroups, daycare homes and centres, and nursery schools, even for children in the earliest years of life. At the same time, researchers have come to recognize that children's friendships can have important functions in their own right, quite apart from the concerns for adult love and approval to which Isaacs referred.

Parents and teachers, for their part, have known for a long time about the potential importance of friendships in children's lives. In particular, children can provide certain resources for their friends that cannot be provided so well by adults. Three ways in which children serve distinctive functions for one another are by providing opportunities for the learning of social skills, by facilitating social comparisons, and by fostering a sense of group belonging.

'Social skills' refer to a wide range of techniques for establishing and managing social interactions and relationships. These skills include the ability to communicate successfully, which in turn necessitates the ability to imagine oneself in the other person's role. Parents often make communication too easy for their own children. They interpret the child's wishes on the basis of incomplete utterances, and they rush to satisfy the child's inferred wants without requiring the child to spell out her intentions explicitly. Children do not have such psychic abilities, and they do not allow their peers the luxury of being cryptic. Relationships with peers can make unique contributions to the learning of many other social skills, including techniques of engaging others in interaction, of tact, and of dealing with conflict. Whereas children can learn from their interactions with their parents how to get along in one sort of social hierarchy – that of the family – it is from their interactions with peers that they can best learn how to survive among equals in a wide range of social situations.

Relationships with one's peers also provide a context in which children can meaningfully compare themselves to others. In encounters between children, such utterances as 'My picture is better than yours', 'Who can run faster – me or you?' and 'Let's see who can jump higher' are frequently heard. These statements, questions, and challenges may at first seem to suggest that children's society is a highly competitive one. On further examination, however, such encounters may be seen as reflecting not so much rivalry as the universal human need to evaluate oneself through comparisons with others.[2] The link between friendship and the opportunity for such comparisons is revealed in the following encounter between two three-year-olds:

(Steven and Claudia stand near the sandbox and hug each other affectionately.)
Steven: You're bigger than me – right, Claudia?
(They turn and stand back to back, measuring themselves. Claudia is in fact taller than Steven.)
Claudia: We're growing up.
Steven: Yeah. I'm almost as big as you, right? I'm gonna grow *this* big, right? (He stretches his arms far apart.)
Claudia: Me too.
Steven: I'm going to grow up to the sky! I'm going to grow *that* high! (He jumps in the air.)
Claudia: Me too.
(Steven and Claudia then go to the nearby sink and pretend to wash each other's hair.)

Psychologists and psychiatrists have argued convincingly that social comparison is necessary for people to develop a valid sense of their own identity.[3] Adults are so different from children on most dimensions that they are relatively useless as comparison points. As an early childhood educator, Katherine H. Read, writes, 'We must measure ourselves against others who are like us, finding our strengths and facing our weaknesses, winning some acceptance and meeting some rejection ... A favourable family situation helps us to feel secure, but experiences with our own age group help to develop an awareness of ourselves and of social reality which family experience alone cannot give.'[4]

Finally, even in early childhood, children already have a strong need for a sense of group belonging, which can be fulfilled only by friendships with their peers. One way in which this need manifests itself is through acts of exclusivity. For example, Jennifer and Alison are putting felt objects on a board when Ruth comes up and puts on an object herself.

> *Jennifer* (to Ruth, sharply): I want to do that myself.
> *Alison*: She wants to do that herself.
> *Jennifer*: I only want to be with Alison.
> *Alison*: Yeah, me!
> (Ruth remains unruffled and later puts another object up on the board.)
> *Jennifer*: Don't put two up. No! You *cannot* stay here with me. I want to play with Alison. (To Alison:) I'm playing with you.

Such exclusivity, which is extremely common in groups of children, can often be understood as a way in which group membership is underlined and confirmed.[5] In this nursery school class, Ricky was unique in that he almost never excluded others from his activities. This was probably because Ricky was also unique in feeling a secure sense of belonging with a large number of other children in the class. The security that comes from a sense of group belonging, however, is different from the security that comes from attachments to parents.

Children, then, provide valuable social resources to one another, and these do not duplicate what is obtained from parents. These unique functions of friendship extend through childhood and into adulthood. Sociologist Robert S. Weiss has noted that adults' relationships tend to be specialized in the resources they provide.[6] We typically obtain emotional security from a single close relationship, often with a husband or wife, and we gain a sense of community from relationships with friends, neighbours, and colleagues. None of these sources of provisions can routinely substitute for the others. A network of friends cannot do much to compensate for the loss of a close attachment, whether through death or desertion. Conversely, the presence of an emotional attachment cannot alleviate the loneliness that people experience when they lack a network of friends or colleagues.[7] Our observations of young children make clear that this specialization of relationships begins early in life.

In a series of influential lectures delivered in the 1940s, the psychiatrist Harry Stack Sullivan endorsed the view that relationships with parents and with friends play distinct roles for children. He suggested that a crucial function of children's friendships is to correct some of the peculiar and potentially harmful views of social life that children are likely to have gained from their early interaction with parents:

> Take, for example, the child who has been taught to expect everything, who has been taught that his least wish will be of importance to the parents, and that any obscurities in expressing what he is after will keep them awake nights trying to anticipate and satisfy his alleged needs. Now picture what happens to that child when he goes to school . . .[8]

It is only through interaction with his peers, Sullivan maintained, that such an overly indulged child can be saved from social maladjustment in adult life. The same is true for the child who rules her parents as a 'petty tyrant' and the child who has been taught by her parents to be completely self-effacing and obedient. 'These are just a few of the many greatly handicapping patterns of dealing with authority which the home permits or imposes on the child,' Sullivan wrote. 'All these children, if they did not undergo very striking change in the juvenile era, would be almost intolerable ingredients, as they grew up, in a group of any particular magnitude.'[9] Sullivan pointed to 'the juvenile era', approximately the years between five and nine, as the time when these handicapping conditions of the home could be – and, for the child's sake, had better be – rectified through interaction with peers in school. It now seems clear, however, that children can serve similar functions for one another as early as ages three and four, and quite possibly even earlier than that.

David is the sort of overly indulged child whom Sullivan had in mind. During his first three years of life, he learned from his parents to expect praise for whatever he did. Tony, although he is David's closest friend, does not feel the need to indulge him to such an extent:

> (David and Tony are sitting together at the drawing table.)
> *David*: Do you like my drawing?
> *Tony*: No.
> *David*: You have to like it.
> *Tony*: I don't have to like it if I don't want to.
> *David*: Why?
> *Tony*: I don't like it, that's why.

One may hope that from a series of such encounters with his friend, David will obtain a more accurate picture not only of his public appeal as an artist but also of the degree of approval he can expect from others.

Given that children's friendships serve these functions, can we assume that the nature of a child's friendships will have an enduring impact on his or her social adjustment in later life? Sullivan believed that children's friendships – or their absence – would indeed have such long-term effects. He noted, for example, that those of his adult male patients who were extremely uncomfortable in their business or social dealings with other men had all lacked opportunities to form close friendships as pre-adolescents. Sullivan was convinced that the failure to have a childhood 'chum' created a social deficit that could not be remedied in later life. His observation, coming as it does from his personal impressions of clinical cases, cannot be taken as strong evidence for the likelihood of such effects. But recent studies have provided more systematic evidence of the possible long-term effects of children's friendships. One group of researchers found that ratings of eight-year-old children by their classmates were related to whether or not these children had psychiatric difficulties over the next eleven to thirteen years. Those children who were to develop psychiatric problems were relatively likely to have been scorned and disparaged by their eight-year-old peers.[10] Another longitudinal study found links between pre-adolescent boys' and girls' patterns of friendship and whether they were rated by researchers as 'warm' or 'aloof' in their social relationships at age thirty.[11]

The psychologists who conducted these studies would be among the first to admit that their correlational data do not establish conclusively that the nature of the children's friendships actually played a role in *causing* the later developments. And it would surely be reckless to make confident predictions about Ricky's and Danny's later social relationships on the basis of their nursery school friendships. There is no reason to believe that the lack of satisfactory peer relationships in early childhood will create deficits that cannot be reversed by later experience. Nevertheless, the longitudinal studies give some credence to our intuitions about children's friendships: by providing opportunities for the learning of social skills, for social comparison, and for the establishment of a sense of group belonging, these early relationships have effects that will reverberate – even if not in wholly predictable ways – in later life.

In fact, few parents and teachers really need to be convinced that friendships are important for their children.

On the contrary, parents and teachers – especially in middle-class America – already seem to be convinced of the importance of 'relating to others', to the point where a quiet child who prefers to spend a good deal of time by himself is likely to be regarded as a problem. And this concern, as David Riesman notes in *The Lonely Crowd*, is transmitted to children even in the earliest years of life. In our 'other-directed' society, Riesman argues, parents make their children feel guilty not so much for the violation of inner standards, as in the previous era, but for the failure to make friends. Teachers aid and abet this parental influence with their focus on 'social adjustment' in the pre-school or grade school classroom. As a result, children develop a concern for making friends that sometimes becomes an obsession. When asked how she would feel if she didn't have any friends, one eight-year-old girl replied, 'I'd feel like killing myself ... I'd make friends even with King Kong.'[12]

Riesman's indictment of our overemphasis on peer relationships must be taken very seriously. With the passion for popularity, he argues, comes a tendency to conform to peer-group standards that can undermine much else that is of value in children's lives, including individual skills, tastes, ideals, and commitments. Parents become most likely to notice – and to lament – the oppressive aspects of peer culture as their children enter adolescence, but by that time it may be too late to do much about it. And, paradoxically, an overemphasis on 'relating to others' can even have the effect of suppressing friendships themselves, substituting a superficial sort of congeniality for real intimacy.

My goal in this book, then, is not to advocate 'relating to others' as a general good; nor is it to argue that children need lots of friends if they are to be happy. We need to respect the different social needs and styles of different children, including the real need that many children have for privacy and solitude. Certainly the quality of children's social relationships is more important than their quantity.

We must also resist the temptation to romanticize intimate friendships. Children's close friendships can have undesirable effects as well as desirable ones. Through their relationships with one another, children are likely to learn not only how to get along with others but also how to reject others ('You can't play with us'), to stereotype them ('There's dummy Dwayne'), and to engage in regressive or antisocial behaviour. Intimate friendships give rise not only to self-acceptance, trust, and rapport, but also to insecurity, jealousy, and resentment. The fact of the matter is that children's closest friendships manifest all of the prominent features of close relationships among adults, including their destructive as well as their constructive elements. Perhaps the biggest difference between children's and adults' interactions is that children tend to be more straightforward. Throughout the course of childhood, in large measure as a consequence of their interactions with one another, children learn the 'skill' of tactical deviousness – and, inevitably, the degree of self-deception that goes along with it. Rather than serving as a panacea for the ills of human social life, then, children's relationships themselves mirror these ills.

But the fact that children's friendships can be harmful only serves to underline their importance. Friends do matter. Friends serve central functions for children that parents do not, and they play a critical role in shaping children's social skills and their sense of identity. Children's experiences with their friends may also have major effects on their later development, including their orientations towards friendship and love as adults. Just as important, friendships are likely to be central to the quality of children's lives. Danny may well turn out to be just as successful as Ricky in his later social relationships. Nevertheless, the difference between a child with close friendships and a child who wants to make friends but is unable to, can be the difference between a child who is happy and a child who is distressed in one large area of life.

In light of both the positive values and the potential dangers of children's friendships, it is important for us to learn as much as we can about them. Especially in the years since 1970, behavioural scientists have made substantial progress in this endeavour. My purpose in this book is to review and integrate what we now know or suspect about children's friendships – the forms they take, the factors that influence them, and their place in children's lives.

2/The Earliest Friendships

My son Elihu's first playgroups, launched when he was eight months old, were peculiarly solitary affairs. Four infants – three of them still crawlers, one beginning to walk – were placed in a living room and instructed by their mothers to get to know each other. That is, after all, what a playgroup is for. Unconcerned about these parental designs, the babies ignored one another. They would occasionally look at one another with what seemed to be mild interest. But the interest was never sustained for more than a few seconds. Instead, the babies divided most of their time between two sorts of activities – boldly exploring the room, furniture, and available toys, and cautiously retreating to their mothers as a base of security.

Even at the earliest sessions, however, there were isolated instances in which one baby approached and made physical contact with another. For example (from my original notes): 'Vanessa takes Elihu by surprise by crawling to him, screaming, and pulling his hair. Elihu looks bewildered. Then he starts to cry and crawls to his mother to be comforted.' Such episodes of hair pulling, poking, and pawing when the babies were eight and nine months old did not appear to involve hostile intent. Instead, they seemed to reflect the babies' interest in exploring one another as physical objects. When Elihu crawled over to another baby's stroller and started to bend the passenger's nose, his actions and manner were indistinguishable from the way in which he handled toy animals, bath toys, and other objects that interested him.

The babies' curiosity about physical objects also led to another sort of contact at this age: 'Elihu crawls over to Jonathan, who is jingling a set of plastic keys, and takes the keys from him. Jonathan tries to take the keys back but doesn't succeed. He retreats to his mother, whimpering softly.' In this instance of 'object-centred contact', Elihu did not have the slightest desire to interact with Jonathan; the jingling keys were what had attracted his attention. The fact that another baby was doing the jingling was irrelevant.

The experience of Elihu and his first playmates corresponds to detailed observations that have been made of infants' social relations. These studies have shown that the earliest stages of interaction consist of exploring the other baby as a physical object and of object-centred contact, in which babies come into proximity with one another because of their attraction to the same toys or other objects. Babies also commonly engage in 'parallel play', in which they perform similar actions without directly engaging one another. But even though young infants may often play side by side, tug each other's hair and clothes, and handle the same objects, it is not until the last few months of the first year of life that they are likely to show the beginnings of real social interaction.

In 'real social interaction', peers are distinguished from inanimate objects and are related to in special ways – ways that reflect the baby's dawning recognition that the other baby is someone who can both initiate and respond to social behaviours. Once such awareness emerges, it develops at a rapid pace through the second and the early part of the third year. By the time children are two and a half years old, they are able to sustain interactions with one another that contain, in fledgling form, all the basic features of social interaction among older children or adults – sustained attention, turn-taking, and mutual responsiveness. Toddlers also distinguish between familiar and unfamiliar peers, and particular pairs of toddlers may establish distinctive patterns of interaction that we can identify as friendships. In the past decade, behavioural researchers have launched the sort of careful research that allows us, for the first time, to describe these earliest friendships and their antecedents.[1]

Let us return to where we left off, then – the last few months of the first year of life – and continue to trace the development of infants' and toddlers' relations with their peers. It is admittedly difficult to identify 'real social interaction' in a baby who hasn't yet begun to talk; there is a fuzzy boundary between object-centred contact and parallel play, on the one hand, and behaviour that is genuinely social, on the other. Nevertheless, there comes a point, usually around the end of the first year, when babies begin to relate to one another in ways that suggest a new appreciation of their peers' responsive human qualities. When Elihu was eleven and a half months old, he was observed to look at Sarah and hold out a block, as if offering it to her. By the time he was fifteen months old, now as a member of a new playgroup, he quite regularly and unambiguously offered objects to other toddlers. 'Elihu, being carried by his father, arrives at Roger's house with a toy in his hand. Roger's mother opens the door, holding Roger in her arms. Elihu immediately extends the toy towards Roger, while looking at him and making a sound which seems to mean "Here".'

At fifteen months, Elihu continued to touch other children fairly frequently. But these touches had a more social quality than his pokes and pulls of several months earlier. He was more likely to look at the other child's face while he touched, as if to monitor his response. When he saw another toddler in a hotel lobby or on the street, he was likely to run up to him, laughing and shouting excitedly, and then put his hand on the other's back or grasp his arm.

More generally, in the early months of the second year, toddlers begin to behave in an unmistakably social way towards each other. This social behaviour can be most clearly identified by the fact that the toddler looks at the other while smiling, extending an object, or making sounds. Through the course of the second year, this social behaviour becomes more complex. Whereas at first the toddler may look and reach simultaneously, later she will look, wave a toy, smile, and vocalize, all at the same time.[2] For the first time, the toddler may offer objects with what seem to be genuinely good feelings towards the other child; on occasions, when angered, she may hit or even bite the other with genuine hostility. These pieces of socially directed behaviour are an achievement in their own right, and serve as basic building blocks of social interaction.

Edward Mueller and his colleagues have suggested that contacts over toys or other objects serve as the launching points for the development of social interaction among toddlers.[3] Toys are likely to facilitate social interaction both by luring toddlers to a common focus of attention and by requiring them to coordinate their behaviour so that both can make use of a toy. At Matthew's birthday party, Elihu (at thirteen months) saw Maria playing with a 'surprise box' – a contraption that requires the child to push a button, turn a wheel, or flick a switch in order to cause a door to open and an animal's head to pop out. Elihu quickly joined her, and soon the two were busily working side by side, each of them patterning some of their actions after those of the other. Later, Elihu and Maria, neither of whom could yet walk without assistance, toddled around together while holding on to opposite sides of a toy cart. Whenever one of them took a step that propelled the cart in a particular direction, the other had to take a corresponding step in order to stay upright. In these episodes, Elihu and Maria did not look directly at one another in any but the most fleeting way. Nevertheless, the surprise box and the toy cart provided opportunities for the toddlers to make contact with one another, to imitate each other's actions, to take turns, and to coordinate their behaviour.

The fact that objects can help to bring babies into contact does not mean that parents who wish to accelerate their children's social development should rush out to the shops for more toys. In fact, several observers of infant development have argued that toys can also distract infants from direct social interaction. In one study, pairs of ten- to twelve-month-old infants were observed in a playroom, both with and without toys in the room. Although the toys did facilitate object-centred contacts, when toys were not available the infants more often touched one another, smiled and gestured to each other, and duplicated each other's actions.[4] Thus, whereas toys have their social uses, they are apparently not essential props for infant sociability. Even without the mediation of toys, infants seem to be predisposed, perhaps as an evolutionary legacy, to take an interest in one another.

From an initial interest in one another, however, there is still a considerable jump to actual social interchanges between peers – the games and dialogues that are the hallmarks of human 'relating'. Social interchanges, as defined by Mueller, are chains of two or more pieces of socially directed behaviour, with some apparent connection between them. Although such interchanges emerge between parents and infants during the first year of life, they are not observed between peers until the early months of the second year. The first social interchanges may be very brief: 'Elihu (fourteen months old) has a cracker in his hand. Matthew waddles over to him, extends his hand and makes a sound. Elihu looks at Matthew, then breaks off a piece of the cracker and extends it to him. Matthew takes the piece and eats it.' As this episode suggests, toddlers' first social interchanges are likely to reflect their increased sensitivity to the needs and feelings of others. For example, one mother observed the following incident involving her sixteen-month son: 'He comes into the living room and finds a friend (same age) sobbing; he becomes suddenly sober, walks over to friend, pats him, then picks up a toy and gives it to him.'[5]

By the middle of the second year, toddlers – especially if they know each other well – may sometimes engage in longer series of alternating bouts of social behaviour. Mueller gives an example of such an encounter between two well-acquainted toddlers, when they were thirteen and fifteen months old respectively:

> Larry sits on the floor and Bernie turns and looks toward him. Bernie waves his hand and says 'da', still looking at Larry. He repeats the vocalization three more times before Larry laughs. Bernie vocalizes again and Larry laughs again. Then the same sequence of one child saying 'da' and the other laughing is repeated twelve more times before Bernie turns away from Larry and walks off. Bernie and Larry become distracted at times during the interchange. Yet when this happens the partner re-attracts attention either by repeating his socially directed action or by modifying it, as when Bernie both waves and says 'da', reengaging Larry.[6]

By eliciting desired responses from one another in these early social interchanges, toddlers display a new order of mastery over their environment. Earlier in life, infants come to exert control over inanimate objects, which can be made to respond in predictable ways (for example, bouncing a ball) and over parents, who are typically eager to reward the infant's smiles, coos, and gestures with encouraging responses. But another baby is much less predictable than an inanimate object and much less obliging than a parent. Exerting control over another baby's behaviour, therefore, is a distinctly new and notable accomplishment.

Social interchanges between toddlers are especially impressive because they require both mutual interest and the precise coordination of plans and actions. Whereas parents or older siblings are likely to hold up both ends of the conversation with toddlers, toddlers who interact with one another must themselves share the responsibility for the exchange. These requirements are not easy to meet. In groups of toddlers, it is common for one child to make an eloquent bid for the attention of another, while the other child remains unmoved by his efforts or even oblivious to them.[7]

Social interchanges may also be prevented when one child's behaviour is directed towards a peer, but the peer's attention remains centred on an object:

Don (fourteen months old), on the floor having his diapers changed, notes Noah (fifteen months old) beside him. Noah has squatted down and is focused entirely on the toy telephone that Don holds in his hands. Don proceeds to offer the phone five times in succession to Noah. Each time Noah reaches out, but looks only at the phone. Four of the five times, Don pulls the phone back, and Noah still focuses only on the toy. The other time, Noah does take the phone base and begins to play with it. However, Don, still holding the receiver, pulls in the base by the cord connecting the two. Noah does not understand why the toy pops out of his hands![8]

In this episode, Don was able to exert almost total control over Noah's actions, much like a puppeteer pulling the strings of a marionette. Since Noah was concerned only with the telephone, and not with having a reciprocal influence on Don, their interaction remained one-sided.

Because of the need for a precise meshing of social goals and behaviour, it is not surprising that throughout the second year of life only a small proportion of the behaviour of toddlers in groups is devoted to social interchanges. And interchanges involving more than two children at once, which would require truly spectacular feats of coordination, are virtually never seen before the age of two. The bulk of the toddlers' time is usually spent in a combination of solitary activity, contacts with other toddlers over toys, and interactions with parents if they are available.

Nevertheless, social interchanges become more prominent over the course of the second year. Mueller's observations suggest that the best teacher of interaction skills is experience. In playgroups studied by Mueller, toddlers who had had extensive opportunities to play with their peers engaged in more frequent and longer interchanges than toddlers of the same age whose opportunities had been more limited.[9] Extensive interaction with adults or with older brothers and sisters does not seem to be a substitute for experience with children of their own age.[10] Unlike learning to play tennis, when one can usually do best by practising with a more skilled and experienced player, when it comes to learning to interact with others the best method seems to be to practise with those who are as inexperienced as oneself. By practising with peers who share one's own lack of social skill, toddlers are best able to learn to coordinate their behaviour and to pull their own weight in social interaction.

Once they have mastered simple social interchanges, toddlers begin to engage in more complex interactions that involve reciprocal roles, such as throwing and catching a ball, chasing and being chased, or talking on a toy telephone. These games involve role-taking skill – the toddler must keep in mind the specific sort of behaviour she wishes to elicit from the peer and must fashion her own behaviour accordingly. The flowering of language, in the second half of the second year and first half of the third, gives toddlers' interactions new richness. Granted, these first conversations may seem quite meaningless:

Carrying a cookie, Gwen passes by Dwight who is drink-
ing apple juice. She stops, they look at each other. In the
subsequent period of exchanges Gwen repeatedly comments 'juice', 'cookie', 'apple'; to each Dwight responds
with 'huh?' Later in the session, Dwight shows Gwen
the fly-swatter with which he has been playing and vocal-
izes 'fly'. She smiles broadly and responds 'apple?'[11]

Such dialogues, puzzling as they may be to adults, contain
the seeds of the meaningful conversations that children
begin to engage in by the time they are three.[12]

It is in these complex social interchanges, whether or
not they involve conversation, that we are most likely to
identify real friendship among pairs of toddlers. Judith
Rubenstein and Carollee Howes observed the play of eight
pairs of nineteen-month-old toddlers who had become
special friends – they had been visiting at each other's
homes on a one-to-one basis two or three times a week for
periods ranging from four to nineteen months.[13] During
the home observations, these buddies spent over half of the
time interacting with one another, far exceeding the amount
of interaction found in most other studies of toddlers' social
behaviour. When the friends were together, moreover, they
played with their toys more creatively than the same
toddlers did when they were alone. For example, one toddler imitated his friend's idea of jumping from a stool to
the floor; this soon evolved into a game in which the two
friends took turns jumping, looking back and forth at one
another, and shouting happily. Rubenstein and Howes
argue convincingly that friendships provide a rewarding
context in which toddlers help one another to elaborate
and extend their skills with objects.

What factors influence the formation of such friendships? First, the two toddlers must have repeated opportunities to play together. In part this reflects the social ease
that comes with familiarity, which for babies – as for adults

– is more likely to breed comfort than contempt.[14] Especially during the first half of the second year, many toddlers display some degree of wariness towards unfamiliar peers, paralleling the fear of adult strangers they often show in the latter part of the first year. [15] Until the toddler has become familiar with a peer, she is likely to inspect him from a distance or to approach him only tentatively; such caution on the part of one or both toddlers will effectively prevent any extended social interaction. Frequent contact with a child of the same age, especially in one-to-one situations, will eliminate this apprehension. And it may do more: frequent contact is likely to lead the toddler to an appreciation of the pleasurable activities that can be engaged in with the peer, and to an idea of what to expect from the other.

Toddlers' friendships are not simply a matter of familiarity, however. Once the opportunity for contact is provided, toddlers may exhibit strong preferences for certain playmates over others. In one of the pioneering studies of infants' and toddlers' social behaviour, conducted at a Montreal foundling hospital in the early 1930s, Katharine Banham Bridges observed that whereas the nine- and ten-month-olds would accept any responsive child as a playmate, by fourteen months the children began to show preferences.[16] Similarly, observers of playgroups and day-care centres frequently discover that two children consistently gravitate towards one another and take unusual pleasure in one another's company. In some cases, the young friends seem to provide a sense of security for one another, reducing or eliminating the distress they would otherwise feel when temporarily separated from their parents.[17]

Researchers have not yet been able to pinpoint the bases of such preferences among toddlers, but they do have some reasonable speculations. In at least some instances, toddlers may pick up cues from their parents about which peers they should become friendly with. While observing laboratory play sessions consisting of two toddlers and their mothers, Joseph Jacobson noticed that the better the two mothers appeared to hit it off, the more the toddlers seemed to like each other.[18] Parents' friendships may well set such a friendly model or tone for toddlers outside the laboratory as well. The most central basis for toddlers' friendships, however, is probably the existence of similarities between their level of development, their temperaments, and their styles of behaviour. Physically active toddlers appear to enjoy play sessions most when they are paired with physically active peers; there may also be a special rapport between two toddlers who are relatively quiet and reflective. Just as older children and adults are most likely to be drawn to others who share their interests and views of the world, we would expect toddlers to enjoy interaction with others who share their own styles of relating to the environment.

Indeed, the perception of similarity lies at the heart of babies' and toddlers' attraction to their peers more generally. Even young babies distinguish clearly between peers and adults, and they usually relate more positively to unfamiliar peers than to unfamiliar adults. And once toddlers have come to know one another, they are likely to prefer the company of their peers in many situations to the company of their own parents. As Rubenstein and Howes suggest, toddler peers often share an interest in certain activities – such as jumping off a step twenty times in succession – that would probably try the patience of even the most devoted parent. Along with the presence of such shared interests, toddlers seem to develop a special sense of identity with others of their own size and social category. Although the toddler cannot yet articulate her discovery, she nevertheless begins to realize that 'Here is another person like me'.

Beginning with the earliest social responses of infancy, babies direct quite distinct kinds of behaviour towards parents and towards other babies. By the second year of life, parents are typically turned to more often as conversational partners and as bases of security, and peers are turned to more often as partners in running, jumping, and other physical activities.[19] These relationships are likely to be mutually supportive. One recent study finds, for example, that those three-year-olds who have the most secure relationships with their mothers also tend to be the most competent in interactions with peers.[20] Another study suggests that the interaction skills that toddlers acquire through painstaking practice with their peers are then put to good use by these toddlers in sustaining interactions with their parents.[21] Although these studies are steps in the right direction, we still know very little about the ways in which parent–toddler and toddler–toddler relationships are likely to affect one another. Nevertheless, it seems clear that through the course of the second year, toddlers reach for themselves one of the central conclusions I stressed in Chapter 1: parents and peers each provide valuable resources, and these resources complement but do not substitute for one another.

In the first two years of life, babies often form social relationships not only with adults and with peers but also with older siblings or other older children. Such relationships must also count among the child's earliest friendships. In some respects, these cross-age relationships are particularly well-suited to advancing the baby's social skills: the older child – say, a three- or four-year-old – is less imposing than an adult, while at the same time more socially skilled and responsive than a peer. The experience of interacting successfully with older children may also embolden infants and toddlers to launch relationships with peers as well. There is some evidence that babies with older siblings or with regular contact with older children are more likely to initiate social interactions with their peers.[22] (In Chapter 8, we will return to an examination of cross-age relationships as important friendships in their own right.)

The child's earliest friendships, then, stem from closely related developments in the domains of social behaviour (what one does to, for, or with other people) and of social awareness (how these people are subjectively viewed). Babies learn to direct increasingly complex social behaviours towards one another and to coordinate these behaviours in order to construct social interchanges. They also come to make increasingly refined conceptual distinctions – between peers and toys, between peers and adults, and, among peers, between strangers, acquaintances, and friends. By the time they are two years old, children seem to have an initial concept of a 'friend', as a familiar peer from whom one expects particular responses and with whom one engages in a distinctive and enjoyable set of activities. The child's conceptions of friendship, and the behaviours that go along with these conceptions, continue to develop. But the roots of these later developments are firmly planted in the first two years of life.

3/What Is a Friend?

We're friends now because we know each other's names
– Tony, age three and a half

Friends don't snatch or act snobby, and they don't argue
or disagree. If you're nice to them, they'll be nice to you
– Julie, age eight

A friend is someone that you can share secrets with at 3 in
the morning with Clearasil on your face – Deborah,
age thirteen

The friendship we have in mind is characterized by
mutual trust; it permits a fairly free expression of emo-
tion; it allows the shedding of privacies (although not
inappropriately); it can absorb, within limits, conflict
between the pair; it involves the discussion of personally
crucial themes, it provides occasions to enrich and en-
large the self through the encounter of differences –
Elizabeth Douvan and Joseph Adelson, adults

As these statements illustrate,[1] people have widely
differing notions of what a friend is and of the nature of
friendship. In his second week at nursery school, three-
year-old Dwayne plays with Philip for the first time and
minutes later runs around the yard shouting 'We're
friends!' Thirteen-year-old Deborah, in contrast, might

spend months getting to know a classmate, gradually extending the range and intimacy of their conversations, before deciding that their relationship merits the label of friendship. Some observers may conclude that young children's notions of friendship are so different from the conceptions held by older children, adolescents, and adults that it is misleading to consider them as variations of the same concept. From this point of view, when pre-schoolers talk about their friends, they are really referring to their playmates, which is a rather different sort of thing. My own view is that the use of the word 'friend' by children of different ages nicely reflects the common functions of peer relationships for people of all ages. Both three-year-old Dwayne and thirteen-year-old Deborah are referring to nonfamilial relationships which are likely to foster a feeling of belonging and a sense of identity; it seems quite appropriate that they choose to use the same word.

It is clear, however, that the ways in which people reason about friendship change over the course of childhood. Moreover, there appear to be some basic consistencies among individuals in the nature of this change.

The most systematic research on children's understandings of friendship is being conducted by Robert Selman and his colleagues at the Harvard Graduate School of Education. Selman has patterned both his theoretical approach and his research style on the model of the Swiss psychologist Jean Piaget. He follows Piaget in taking as his central concern the progressively developing mental structures that characterize children's social thought. He also follows Piaget in his method of documenting these mental structures – the clinical interview, in which the interviewer probes deeply and resourcefully to capture the child's own understanding of her social world. Selman has adopted this procedure to assess the 'friendship awareness' of both normal and emotionally disturbed children, from early childhood through adolescence.[2] On the basis of this work, it is possible for us to identify two sharply contrasting stages of children's conceptions of friendship.

The young child, from about age three to five, characteristically views friends as 'momentary physical playmates' – whomever one is playing with at a particular time. Children at this stage do not have a clear conception of an enduring relationship that exists apart from specific encounters. Young children may in fact *have* enduring relationships with others, but they typically conceive of them only in terms of momentary interaction. In addition, children at this stage reflect only on the physical attributes and activities of playmates, rather than on psychological attributes such as personal needs, interests, or character traits. In contrast, the older child – by age eleven or twelve – comes to view close friendships as involving 'intimate and mutual sharing'. Children at this later stage regard friendship as a relationship that takes shape over a period of time. Friends are seen as providers of intimacy and support. The child realizes that, to achieve these ends, close friends need to be psychologically compatible – to share interests and to have mutually agreeable personalities.

To gain a fuller understanding of the contrast between these two stages of reasoning about friendship, let us compare the ways in which younger and older children reflect upon certain central issues: what sorts of people make good friends, how friendships are formed, and the nature of closeness and intimacy.

What sorts of people make good friends? For the young child who views friendship in terms of momentary interactions, the most important qualification for friendship is physical accessibility. When asked what sort of person makes a good friend, pre-schoolers are likely to provide such answers as 'Someone who plays a lot' or 'Someone who lives in Watertown'.[3] Young children are also likely to focus on specific physical actions. Steven tells me, for example, that Craig is his friend because 'he doesn't take things away from me'. Conversely, Jake is not his friend because 'he takes things away from me'. For children at this level, moreover, one's own desires may be seen as a sufficient basis for friendship. When you ask a young child why a certain other child is his friend, the most common reply is 'Because I like him'. Attempts to probe more deeply are likely to frustrate both the researcher and the child:

ZR: Why is Caleb your friend?
Tony: Because I like him.
ZR: And why do you like him?
Tony: Because he's my friend.
ZR: And why is he your friend?
Tony (speaking each word distinctly, with a tone of mild disgust at the interviewer's obvious denseness): Because ... I ... choosed ... him ... for ... my ... friend.

Children at this stage do not make reference to psychological attributes of friends; at most, they will resort to such stereotypical descriptions as 'she's nice' or 'he's mean'.

Older children are aware of other sorts of qualifications for friendship. Instead of focusing on physical accessibility, they are likely to emphasize the need for psychological compatibility. One aspect of this rapport is the sharing of outlooks and interests. When asked why Jimmy was his friend, thirteen-year-old Jack explained: 'We like the same kinds of things. We speak the same language.'[4] Children at this level of social awareness also realize that compatibility is not to be equated with similarity. 'Good friends sort of fit together,' thirteen-year-old Alan said. 'They don't have to be exactly alike, but if one is strong in something the other can be weak and he may be good at something else.'[5]

How are friendships formed? For children who view friendship in terms of momentary physical interaction, the way to form a friendship is simply to play with the other child. When asked how one should go about making friends, younger children are likely to provide such answers as 'Move in next door', 'Tell him your name', and 'Just go up and ask her to play'. From this perspective, the barriers to making friends are physical rather than psychological. A four-year-old interviewed by Selman explained things this way:

> *Interviewer*: Is it easy or hard to make friends?
> *Child*: Hard, because sometimes if you wave to the other person, they might not see you wave, so it's hard to get that friend.
> *Interviewer*: What if they see you?
> *Child*: Then it's easy.[6]

Older children, who view friendships as relationships that continue beyond single encounters, view the process as more complicated. Although they recognize that people may sometimes 'hit it off' immediately, these children believe that friendships can best be established gradually, as people find out about one another's traits, interests, and values. 'You don't really pick your friends,' thirteen-year-old Jack reported. 'It just grows on you. You find out that you can talk to someone, you can tell them your problems, when you understand each other.'[7]

The nature of intimacy. For the young child, the question of what constitutes closeness translates into the question of what distinguishes a best friend from other friends. And when such a distinction is made, it is in strictly quantitative terms – whatever you do with a friend, you simply do more of it with a best friend: 'If you *always* visit, you're best friends.' Pre-school children may in fact have best friends with whom they interact in ways that seem qualitatively unique to the adult observer. Nevertheless, children who view friendship in terms of momentary physical interactions seem unable to reflect on the special nature of such friendships.

Children who view friendship as a mutual relationship, in contrast, can reflect specifically on the nature of intimacy. Closeness is defined in terms of the degree of understanding that has been built up between two friends, the extent to which they trust each other with personal thoughts and feelings, and the extent to which they are concerned with one another's welfare. A fifteen-year-old boy put it this way:

> A really tight friendship is when you start to really care about the person. If he gets sick, you kind of start worrying about him – or if he gets hit by a car. An everyday friend, you say, I know that kid, he's all right, and you don't really think much of him. But a close friend you worry about more than yourself. Well, maybe not more, but about the same.[8]

This conception of intimacy between friends is remarkably similar to the ways in which philosophers and psychologists have typically defined love.[9] In his discussion of the friendships of late childhood, Harry Stack Sullivan made this equation explicitly: 'If you will look very closely at one of your children when he finally finds a chum, you will discover something very different in the relationship – namely, that your child begins to develop a new sensitivity to what matters in another person. And this is not in the sense of "what should I do to get what I want", but instead "what should I do to contribute to the happiness or to support the prestige and feeling of worthwhileness of my chum" ... This change represents the beginning of something very like full-blown psychiatrically defined *love*.'[10]

Along what path do children progress from a view of friendship as momentary physical interaction to a view of friendship as mutual sharing and intimacy? Is there a sudden flash of social insight, akin to the rapid vocabulary growth of the second year of life or to the height spurt that accompanies puberty? Surely this is not the way it happens. One view of the way it does happen, taken by Selman – with due credit to Piaget – is that social awareness develops in a series of stages, each of which involves a reorganization of mental elements by the child. The two stages of reasoning about friendship that we have examined are labelled 'Stage 0' and 'Stage 3'. To get from Stage 0 to Stage 3, the child progresses through two intermediate stages. In Stage 1, most often characteristic of children between the ages of about six and eight, the child conceives of friendship as 'one-way assistance'. A friend is a person who does things that please you; accordingly, friends must become aware of one another's likes and dislikes. At this stage, however, there is still no awareness of the reciprocal nature of friendship. This comes at Stage 2, which is most often characteristic of children between the ages of about nine and twelve. For the first time, friendship is understood as a two-way street in which each friend must adapt to the needs of the other. In Stage 2, however, children's awareness of reciprocity remains focused on specific incidents rather than on the friendship itself, as an enduring social relationship. For this reason, Selman labels this the stage of 'fairweather cooperation'. It is only in the transformation from Stage 2 to Stage 3 that children, by now typically in late childhood or early adolescence, come to reflect on issues of intimacy and mutuality in a continuing relationship.

Thus Selman describes a stepladder progression in children's friendship awareness. Children climb the ladder, stopping to rest for a while at each rung – in part, presumably, to consolidate the new level of interpersonal awareness that they have achieved – before going on. Other researchers, while confirming this general progression, doubt that the stages are as distinct as Selman's scheme suggests. Whether the progression is like ascending a stepladder or a gradually inclining ramp, however, it involves steady movement along three dimensions of social understanding.

First, there is a progression in the child's ability to take other people's point of view, comparable to the broadening of visual perspective-taking ability that takes place in early childhood.[11] Whereas young children assume that everyone else sees physical objects in precisely the same way that they do, they later come to recognize that different people will see a particular object in different ways, depending on their physical vantage point. An analogous progression takes place in the domain of social understanding. At first, children view friendship in a one-sided and egocentric way, solely in terms of what a friend can do for them. A friend is a friend because 'I like him' or 'He plays with me' or 'I want him to be my friend'. Only at later stages do children become capable of figuratively standing back and taking the other person's viewpoint ('She doesn't like it when I act too wild') and, still later, a third-person perspective on their relationships, with an appreciation of interlocking needs and provisions ('We share a lot of the same values'). Thus the developing ability to take another person's point of view can be seen as a mark of both cognitive and social maturing.

Second, there is a shift from viewing people only as physical entities to viewing people as psychological entities as well.[12] When younger children are asked to describe their friends or acquaintances, they concentrate on physical attributes and activities: 'Andy's got red hair and he always wears cowboy boots.' As children grow older they begin to supplement such concrete descriptions with abstract concepts that refer to behavioural dispositions:

'He's a big show off.'[13] Children also become increasingly likely to provide their own psychological explanations of other people's behaviour, such as 'Because he is black he is very defensive' or 'She says bad things about other people so you'll be closer to her'.[14] Children, like adults, are everyday psychologists, and their psychologizing becomes more sophisticated – even if not always more accurate – over the course of childhood. In accord with these changes, appraisals of the psychological attributes of others become increasingly important aspects of friendship.

Third, children's conceptions of friendship reflect a shift from viewing social relationships as momentary interactions to viewing them as social systems that endure over some period of time. In terms of a distinction suggested by Erving Goffman, young children conceptualize their commerce with others only as *encounters*, whereas older children become able to conceptualize *relationships*.[15] Following a fight, for example, a young child may be quick to shout 'We're not friends!' An older child, like this twelve-year-old, takes a longer view:

> You have known your friend so long and loved him so much, and then all of a sudden you are so mad at him, you say, I could just kill you and you still like each other, because you have always been friends and you know in your mind you are going to be friends in a few seconds anyway.[16]

These three developmental progressions have a basic theme in common: there is a shift in focus from the concrete to the abstract – from observable, here-and-now characteristics of people and their behaviour to inferred, underlying characteristics. These progressions in social understandings are made possible, in part, by parallel progressions from concrete to abstract reasoning in a child's intellectual development.[17] But intellectual development alone cannot account for the specific content of children's conceptions of friendship. What is it that causes children to transform their notions of friendship from momentary interaction to one-way assistance, from fairweather cooperation to shared intimacy? One possibility is that it is chiefly a matter of cultural learning, from the models and formulas provided by adults, older children, and the mass media: 'You have to share with your friends', 'Mummy's talking on the phone to her best friend', 'Batman and Superman are Superfriends – they never let each other down'. From this standpoint, the child's changing conceptions of friendship are a series of successively closer approximations to the views of friendship held in a particular culture. It must be acknowledged that Selman and other researchers have derived their descriptions from studies of children in Western societies, usually from middle-class backgrounds. We can safely assume that at least some of the details of these progressions tend to be different among children in non-Western cultures – where, for example, friendship may be based to a large degree on formalized arrangements such as blood brotherhood.[18] Moreover, within the United States, as we shall see in Chapter 9, there is reason to believe that children from different social backgrounds come to have somewhat different conceptions of friendship.

Without denying the likelihood of such differences, however, most developmental psychologists believe that the principal architect of social understanding is not the child's culture but the child himself. According to this 'constructivist' view, as espoused by both Piaget and Sullivan, children work out for themselves what social relationships are all about on the basis of their actual encounters with others. Through their interactions with peers, children discover that other children are similar to them in some respects and different in others. And as children attempt to cooperate with one another, they discover that the coordination of behaviour requires an appreciation of the other's capabilities, desires, and values. At first, these 'discoveries' remain implicit and unexamined. Gradually, however, children integrate and organize what they have learned, and are led to increasingly sophisticated understandings of social relationships. Talking openly about conflicts may be one particularly valuable way to further one's understanding of friendship.

Although the constructivist view is widely held, there is still no systematic research that succeeds in pinning down the ways in which specific experiences lead to transformations in children's social awareness.[19] Even in the absence of such research, however, the constructivist view can help us to make sense out of several observations about children's social understandings that might otherwise be puzzling.

First, the constructivist view helps to make clear that there is no inevitable relation between a child's age and his or her level of interpersonal understanding. Whereas almost all children begin to walk within a limited age range – between about nine and fourteen months – there is much greater variation in the ages at which children begin to reason about friendship at particular levels. Unlike walking, the development of social understanding depends on both developing intellectual skills, which may vary widely among individuals, and on specific social experiences, which vary even more widely. As a result, we should be sure not to rely on chronological age as an unfailing guide of children's social understanding.

The constructivist view also helps us to see why there are almost always discrepancies between how children answer questions about friendship and how the same children relate to their friends in practice. For example, young children who characteristically view friendship as momentary physical interactions may still demonstrate an ability to work out compromises that suggests a clear practical awareness of the give-and-take of relationships. 'I'll live with you there,' one pre-school boy told a girl who wanted him to play house again, 'but I'll work here, and I'm working now' – and he went on building with blocks.[20] As Piaget emphasizes, 'Thought always lags behind action and cooperation has to be practised for a very long time before it can be brought fully to light by reflective thought.'[21]

Finally, the constructivist view accommodates the fact that there are often apparent inconsistencies in children's responses to questions about friendship. My nephew Larry, at twelve, explained why Mark was his best friend in terms of the sharing of outlooks and interests: 'We're both short, we're the same smartness, and we like the same sports.' Such awareness of the psychological bases of compatibility is characteristic of Stage 3 reasoning in Selman's scheme. But when I asked Larry what would lead people who were best friends not to be friends any more, he could think only of the possibilities that one of them moved away or transferred to another school, reflecting a physicalistic conception of friendship that is more characteristic of Selman's Stage 0. The notion that friends can grow apart because of changing outlooks or interests did not occur to Larry, who had not yet had much experience with the ending of friendships. Such 'inconsistencies' are to be expected, once we recognize that the child's conceptions are derived from interpretations of concrete experiences rather than from logical analysis of friendships in the abstract.

This discussion of children's progression towards increasingly 'advanced' conceptions of friendship may seem to imply that, by the time we become adults, we all reason about friendship in thoroughly sophisticated, humane, and logical terms. The conception of friendship by two psychologists that I quoted at the start of this

chapter – with its mutual trust, absorption of conflict, and
opportunity for self-enrichment – is one definition of this
ideal endpoint. It is worthwhile to ask, however, whether
most adults typically conceive of friendship in such terms.
The fact is that they do not. When adults of varying ages
are asked to explain the basis of their close friendships,
they mention a wide range of factors, including physical
proximity ('Because we're neighbours'), likeability ('He is a
good companion'), similarity of outlooks ('We have the
same interests ... in religion and the way we look at
things'), trust ('She listens and you know it is not going any
further'), and reciprocal help and support ('I know that if
I ever needed help with anything I could always go to
her').[22] The reasoning behind these descriptions runs the
gamut from Stage 0 to Stage 3 and beyond. Adults'
descriptions of an 'ideal close relationship' reflect almost
the same range and diversity.

My point is not that adults frequently reason like
children about friendship. It is, rather, that people do not
in fact progress towards more advanced levels of social
awareness in an ever-upward climb towards an ideal, with
each 'higher' level, once attained, replacing the lower levels
already passed. Instead, as Selman and others have noted,
lower stages are not discarded but are built upon and
remain available for future use in specific situations. It is
interesting to note, in this connection, that both children
and adults tend to reason in more sophisticated ways about
their deepest friendships and loves than about casual
relationships. Indeed, one's view of any close relationship, as it progresses from first meetings to intimacy, may
have to go through the very same stages – albeit in a
shorter time period – as do conceptions of friendship
through the course of childhood.[23]

What, then, is a friend? Philosophers and psychologists
can provide their own definitions, but these are not

entirely adequate to our purposes. Friendship, in the sense that it matters to us, is what a child makes it out to be. Whether Billy views Sean as 'someone I play with in school' or as 'someone I can trust – and who can trust me' will inevitably have a major impact on the way in which Billy proceeds to conduct his relationship with Sean. And these conceptions contain important clues about how Billy is likely to navigate relationships with other children as well. If we are interested in understanding a child's friendships, therefore, we must do our best to understand them in the child's own terms.

4/The Skills of Friendship

I began this book with an account of two boys in the same pre-school class – Ricky, who made many friends, and Danny, who made none. Ricky's greater ability to make friends could not have been predicted from the two boys' physical or intellectual characteristics. But Ricky had mastered to an impressive degree the social skills needed to establish and maintain friendships. These skills include the abilities to gain entry into group activities, to be approving and supportive of one's peers, to manage conflicts appropriately, and to exercise sensitivity and tact. They are subtle skills, by no means easy to learn, and the fact that most children ultimately succeed in acquiring them is itself one of the most remarkable aspects of social development.

Consider, first, the immediate problem confronting a child who enters a new group and wants to join other children in their play. During their first days in a new pre-school setting, children frequently avoid their peers and instead hover nervously on the sidelines.[1] As they become more familiar with their environment, the newcomers may try to approach other children. But these attempts – like Danny's – are not likely to succeed until the child has accumulated a repertoire of tactics for entering groups, complete with implicit rules about how and when a certain ploy can be used most effectively.

William Corsaro offers the following example of the 'access strategies' of four-year-olds in nursery school:

Two girls, Jenny and Betty, are playing around a sandbox in the outside courtyard of the school. I am sitting on the ground near the sandbox watching. The girls are putting sand in pots, cupcake pans, bottles and teapots . . . Another girl, Debbie, approaches and stands near me observing the other two girls. Neither Jenny nor Betty acknowledges her presence. Debbie does not speak to me or the other girls, and no one speaks to her. After watching for some time (5 minutes or so) she circles the sandbox three times and stops again and stands near me. After a few more minutes of watching, Debbie moves to the sandbox and reaches for a teapot in the sand. Jenny takes the pot away from Debbie and mumbles, 'No.' Debbie backs away and again stands near me observing the activity of Jenny and Betty. Then she walks over next to Betty, who is filling the cupcake pan with sand. Debbie watches Betty for just a few seconds, then says: 'We're friends, right? We're friends, right, Betty?'

Betty, not looking up at Debbie and while continuing to place sand in the pan, says, 'Right.'

'I'm making coffee,' Debbie says to Betty.

'I'm making cupcakes,' Betty replies.

Betty turns to Jenny and says, 'We're mothers, right, Jenny?'

Jenny replies, 'Right.'

The three 'mothers' continue to play together for twenty more minutes, until the teachers announce cleanup time.[2]

Debbie's persistent effort to join the group illustrates a variety of strategies. At first Debbie merely places herself in the area of the interaction, a strategy that Corsaro calls 'nonverbal entry'. When this tactic gets no response,

Debbie proceeds to 'encircle' the area. When this strategy, too, is ignored, she enters the area directly and produces 'similar behaviour' (she picks up a teapot). And when this attempt is rebuffed, Debbie switches to a verbal strategy, making a direct 'reference to affiliation' ('We're friends, right?'). After Betty responds positively to this move, Debbie once again produces behaviour similar to that of the others, this time explicitly describing it ('I'm making coffee'). At this point, Debbie's attempt to join the group finally succeeds. Betty responds in a way that includes Debbie in the activity ('We're mothers'), and the three now play together for some time.

Corsaro notes that nursery school children rarely use more direct verbal access strategies, such as saying 'Hi', 'What ya doing?' or 'Can I play?' One likely reason is that such direct approaches call for a direct response by the approached children, and this response is very likely to be negative. Once two or more children have structured and defined for themselves a particular activity, whether it is making cupcakes or blasting off in a spaceship, they often 'protect' their activity by excluding any outsiders who might dare to request entry. Sometimes this exclusive stance is established even before the activity begins. For example:

> (David, Josh, and Jonah are in the sandbox together.)
> *David* (to Josh): Will you help me make some soup?
> *Josh*: Yeah – and Jonah can't play, right?

Unless the 'outsider' is already a highly accepted group member who has special rights of entry, young children will frequently refuse him admission. A 'Hi' may be ignored, a 'What ya doing?' responded to with 'We're making cupcakes and you're not', and a direct 'Can I play?' answered with an equally direct 'No'. To enter the activity, therefore, the child may have to be cautious and subtle, like Debbie. By first reconnoitring the situation unobtrusively, then quietly joining in the ongoing activity, and finally making direct verbal statements – including the ingratiating 'We're friends, right?' – Debbie was able to include herself in Betty and Jenny's activity without mobilizing their resistance.

On the other hand, direct approaches may be more effective when the child wants to engage a single other child who is not already involved in a group activity. And as children grow older, specific verbal formulas for initiating interaction become more important. In a study of eight- and nine-year-olds, John Gottman and his co-workers asked children to pretend that the researcher was a new child in the class with whom they wanted to make friends.[3] From the children's performance in this role-play situation, the researchers were able to assess their knowledge of friendship-making tactics. Offering greetings ('Hi, Mary'), offering appropriate information ('My favourite sport is basketball'), requesting information ('Where do you live?'), and extending invitations ('Wanna come over to my house some time?') were all scored as reflecting the child's knowledge of how to make friends. The researchers then compared these social-knowledge scores with popularity ratings derived from questions asked of all class members. They found, not surprisingly, that popular children knew more about how to make friends than unpopular children did.

'Knowing how' to make friends is no guarantee of social success, however. Some children may excel on a role-play test of social skills but at the same time may be unable or unwilling to put these skills to practical use. For example, an experience with rejection may lead some children to avoid approaching others for long periods of time; other children will bounce back from rejection much more easily. As Carol Dweck and Therese Goetz suggest, the difference in reactions may depend on the child's

personal explanation of a rejection.[4] Some children tend to
blame any rejection on their own inadequacies ('I'm just
a shy person') and, as a result, do not feel that the
problem can be overcome. Other children will attribute the
same rejection to temporary moods or misunderstandings
('Maybe her mother yelled at her that morning') and will
persist in their efforts to gain acceptance. In this comparison, it is the resilient child who is more likely to
establish friendships.

The skills of friendship include not only the ability to
gain entry into group activities, but also the ability to *be*
a friend – an attentive, approving, and helpful playmate
and associate. Even in the first year of life, children have
distinctive styles of interaction that can make them agreeable or disagreeable to their peers. Lee C. Lee observed
a daycare group of five infants in Ithaca, New York, for
a period of six months, beginning when the infants were all
about nine months old.[5] She found that one of the infants,
Jenny, was by far the best-liked member of the group;
throughout the six-month period, each of the other four
babies approached her most often. Patrick was the least-
liked group member; he was approached least often by
three of the other four infants. On the basis of detailed
observations of each baby, Lee was able to paint a picture
of their contrasting styles of interaction. Jenny was a
responsive, adaptive social partner. She displayed a range
of emotions in her social encounters. And she seldom
terminated social contacts that had been initiated by
others. Patrick, on the other hand, was a belligerent and
unfriendly baby. He frequently grabbed others and was
reluctant to end encounters that he had initiated. But
when others initiated contacts with him, he was passive and
unresponsive. Patrick did not smile, laugh, or otherwise
display positive feelings in a single one of the occasions in
which he was contacted by another baby. To put it bluntly,
Patrick was no fun. Not surprisingly, in light of their

differing styles of response, Jenny continued to be approached by other babies while Patrick was shunned.

There is no strong reason to believe that such differences in the 'likeability' of infants are likely to persist past the second year of life. As children grow older, however, they become capable of producing a wider range of behaviour that may be either rewarding or unrewarding to their peers. In extensive observations of nursery school children, Willard Hartup and his colleagues at the University of Minnesota found that the most popular children – those whom their classmates enjoyed playing with most – were also the ones who most often paid attention to other children, praised them, showed affection, and willingly acceded to their requests. Children who frequently ignored others, refused to cooperate, ridiculed, blamed, or threatened others were most likely to be disliked by their classmates.[6] In short, for a child to be included and accepted, he must also include and accept.

Again, Ricky epitomizes such an inclusive and accepting child. He is an engaging, supportive boy who goes out of his way to involve others in his activities. When Caleb comes out to the big rotating swing, which already has four children on board, Ricky immediately shouts to him, 'You can get on it!' 'It's crowded,' Caleb shouts back. In Ricky's view of things, however, there is always room for one more. 'Someone else wants to get on,' he informs his fellow riders. Then he takes charge of slowing down the swing and shows Caleb where he can climb on. Ricky is a skilful social facilitator, and others like him for it.

It is important to stress, however, that 'friendly' behaviour does not always win friendship. Whether an affectionate act is in fact experienced as rewarding will depend on *how* the affection is expressed and, most important, how it is interpreted by the recipient. While some children must learn to be more outgoing, others must learn to stop 'coming on too strong'. At the beginning of the year, Fiona would regularly run up to other children and hug them effusively. She discovered, to her dismay, that this display of affection usually frightened off the others. She eventually learned that she could do better by approaching others more subtly – for example, by patting them on the arm and suggesting an activity.

What may be, for one child, a show of friendship is not necessarily viewed that way by another. Even gift giving can backfire, if the recipient attributes ignoble motives to the giver. Ann, who began to interact with other children only late in the school year, gave Craig a paper envelope she had made, as a gesture of friendship. Later Craig tells me, 'I'm not going to take it home because it doesn't have a drawing.' 'Why do you think Ann gave it to you?' I ask. 'I don't know. Maybe she doesn't like it either.' Moreover, the same overt behaviour can be regarded as rewarding if it comes from a child one already likes and unrewarding if it comes from a child one already has doubts about. 'I'll tell you why I don't like David,' Rachel explains to me. 'Because he screams around all sorts of places. But I don't mind if Steven screams because he just screams a little bit.'

Studies of nursery school children have also indicated that the best-liked children are not highly dependent on teachers.[7] Ricky often chatted amiably with teachers and generally followed their instructions, but only rarely went to a teacher for help in dealing with routine matters. Danny, in contrast, frequently called for help in a whiny tone of voice and would cry for the teacher whenever he received a minor injury or rebuff. Ricky's lesser dependence on teachers was almost certainly related to his greater ability to be supportive of his classmates. When a child must constantly turn to adults for support and assistance, he is unlikely to have the emotional resources necessary to be rewarding to his peers.

The skills of friendship also include the ability to manage

conflicts successfully. Children learn that it is often valuable to talk out their hurt feelings in order to restore good will. While playing fireman, for example, Josh and Tony managed to offend each other. After a period of sullen silence, the following conversation ensued:

> *Josh*: I'm not going to be your friend, Tony. You're talking mean to me so I'm not going to be your friend.
> *Tony*: You're talking mean to *me*.
> *Josh*: You're calling me names – Bloody Boy, Fire Boy.
> *Tony*: Well, you're not letting me and David play by ourselves.

Once they put these feelings on the table, Josh and Tony quickly restored harmony. 'I can be a fireboy in the fireman game,' Josh declares. 'Let him spray out fires,' Tony orders his other fireman.

In order to maintain friendships in the face of the disagreements that inevitably arise, children must learn to express their own rights and feelings clearly while remaining sensitive to the rights and feelings of others. They must be able to suggest and to accept reasonable compromises, even as they stand up against unreasonable demands. As S. Holly Stocking and Diana Arezzo note, different children may start in different places in their quest for the ability to manage conflict appropriately:

> The overly aggressive child . . . may need to learn how to listen to others without interrupting or putting them down, and how to accept reasonable disagreement gracefully, without anger or attack. The overly submissive child, in turn, may have to learn how to stand up for himself with a definite posture and a calm tone of voice that communicates conviction.[8]

As children become more sensitive to the feelings of their

peers, they also learn the subtle skills of tact that are needed
to maintain friendships. Even four-year-olds may begin to
display such tact, especially in the context of close friendships. When Tony took his pants off to go swimming, for
example, his best friend David inadvertently burst into
laughter. But a moment later, David turned to Tony and
assured him, 'I'm not laughing at you, Tony. I'm laughing
at Neil.' Although this explanation may have involved a
white lie on David's part, it also illustrates his sensitivity
to his friend's feelings and his ability to act in such a way
as to protect them.

I observed a particularly striking example of tact among
four-year-olds in the following conversation between
David and Josh, who were walking together and pretend-
ing to be robots:

> *David*: I'm a missile robot who can shoot missiles out
> of my fingers. I can shoot them out of everywhere –
> even out of my legs. I'm a missile robot.
> *Josh* (tauntingly): No, you're a fart robot.
> *David* (protestingly): No, I'm a missile robot.
> *Josh*: No, you're a fart robot.
> *David* (hurt, almost in tears): No, Josh!
> *Josh* (recognizing that David is upset): And I'm a
> poo-poo robot.
> *David* (in good spirits again): I'm a pee-pee robot.

As in the case of the interaction between David and Tony,
Josh realized that he had said something ('you're a fart
robot') that greatly distressed his friend. He handled the
situation resourcefully by putting himself down as well
('I'm a poo-poo robot'), thus demonstrating that his insult
was not to be taken seriously. David's response to Josh's
move ('I'm a pee-pee robot') indicates that Josh had
appraised the situation accurately and had successfully
saved his friend's feelings.

Acquiring the skills of friendship can be a difficult struggle for the pre-school child, especially if he has not had much previous experience in interacting with other children of his own age without direct adult supervision. Nursery schools often serve as valuable proving grounds for the development of such skills. Although the learning may sometimes be painful or frustrating, children gradually develop both more sophisticated concepts of friendship and more sophisticated techniques for establishing and maintaining such friendships for themselves. The development of communication skills through interaction with one's peers may itself be an important prerequisite for the acquisition of skills specifically related to friendship. In this connection, Danny, who had doting parents but little experience with children of his own age before entering nursery school, probably suffered in his attempts at making friends because of his relatively undeveloped powers of communication. Ricky, in contrast, lived in the same household as several cousins of varying ages and had developed communication skills of an unusually high order. With additional experience, as it turned out, Danny, too, became more successful at making friends. When I revisited him a year after I had concluded my observations of the class, I found that he was interacting much more successfully and was sought out by several of his classmates.

Children, then, acquire social skills not so much from adults as from their interaction with one another. They are likely to discover through trial and error which strategies work and which do not, and later to reflect consciously on what they have learned. While playing with blocks one day, four-year-old Alec remarked to his teacher, 'Remember that day when I gave Colin a truck he needed? That was a very nice thing to do, don't you think, Miss Beyer?'[9] Children also learn social skills from the direct tutelage or examples provided by their peers. When David

whines, 'Gary pushed me,' for example, Josh firmly
advises him, 'Just say stop.' In other instances, children
introduce their friends to one another, help others to
launch joint activities, or show others how to resolve their
conflicts. Rachel is one child who is successful, in her own
soft-spoken way, in promoting good feelings among other
children. For example, she serves as timekeeper while
several other children take turns standing in a special
hiding place. When Claudia occupies the space before it is
her turn, Rachel calls her back to the table where the
timekeeper's hourglass is kept and gently explains, 'Here,
Claudia – when it goes all the way through there it's your
turn, all right?' When all the sand has trickled through,
Rachel happily informs Claudia that her turn has come,
and lets Alison know that her time has run out. One
suspects that such advice and assistance from respected
peers may often be more effective than similar inter-
ventions by teachers or parents.

There are also cases, however, when children need help
from adults in mastering particular skills of friendship.
When children wish to make friends but lack the skills to
do so, vicious circles can be set in motion. The friendless
child must interact with his peers in order to develop the
self-confidence and skills needed for social success. But his
lack of social skills – for example, the inability to approach
other children or the tendency to scare them off – may cut
him off from just such opportunities. In such cases, inter-
vention by parents or teachers may be necessary. One
approach is to steer a friendless child to a particular other
child – sometimes one who also lacks friends – with
whom the adult thinks the child might hit it off. In at
least some cases, such matchmaking can help to give two
withdrawn children an initial and valuable experience of
social acceptance. Another tactic, to which we will return
in Chapter 8, is to pair an older child who is too competitive or aggressive with a younger child to whom he can

relate as a 'big brother' – and, in the process, learn that he can win the approval of others without being a bully.[10]

Psychologists have also developed a variety of training programmes for both pre-school and school-age children. In such programmes, children who have been identified as isolates or outcasts are given a series of sessions which may include demonstrations of specific social skills, opportunities to practise them, and feedback on their performance. In at least some cases, these programmes have been notably successful in increasing the social acceptance of initially isolated children.[11]

Because training programmes tend to be focused on increasing 'social acceptance' or 'popularity', they bring up some troublesome questions of values. Do the programmes really help children develop the capacity for friendship, or are they geared to some 'American' ideal of glib sociability and congeniality that has little to do with real friendship at all? The answer to this question depends both on the details of the programme and on the values of the adults who administer it. In the view of at least some leading practitioners, however, 'The objective of social skills instruction is not to create "popular" or "outgoing" children, but to help youngsters, whatever their personality styles, to develop positive relationships ... with at least one or two other children.'[12] One can also ask whether it is ethically acceptable to impose social skills training on children who have little choice in the matter and who in some instances may not really want to be changed into 'friendlier' people. In the last analysis, though, the most compelling defence for such programmes is that they may be able to increase the child's degree of control over her own life. As Melinda Combs and Diana Arezzo Slaby note, 'A child who has the skills to initiate play and communicate with peers may still choose to spend a good deal of time alone. But that child will be able to interact effectively when she (he) wants to or when the situation requires it.

On the other hand. a socially unskilled child may be alone or "isolated" out of necessity rather than by choice.'[13]

Even without instituting formal training, parents and teachers can make use of similar demonstrations, explanations, and feedback in order to teach the skills of friendship in school or home settings. In making use of such procedures, however, adults must be sensitive to the fine line that exists between help and interference. Although adults have a role to play in teaching social skills to children, it is often best that they play it unobtrusively. In particular, adults must guard against embarrassing unskilled children by correcting them too publicly and against labelling children as shy in ways that may lead the children to see themselves in just that way.[14]

Rather than 'pushing' social skills indiscriminately, adults should respect the real differences between children that motivate some to establish friendly relations with many others, some to concentrate on one or two close friendships, and some to spend a good deal of time by themselves. Children's friendships take many forms and involve different styles of interaction. In our efforts to help children make friends, we should be more concerned with the quality of these friendships than with their quantity.

Adults must also recognize that there are many personal attributes, some of them relatively immutable, which are likely to affect the way a child is viewed by his peers in a particular setting, including physical appearance, athletic prowess, intellectual abilities, and family background.[15] As a result, different children may be best equipped with somewhat different skills of friendship. Finally, adults must be sensitive to events in children's lives that may underlie problems with making and keeping friends. Moving to a new school or neighbourhood may create special difficulties, and so may stressful family events such as divorce.[16] For the most part, as we have seen, children learn the skills of friendship not from adults but from each other. But parents and teachers who are sensitive to individual children's distinctive needs and circumstances can play a crucial role in facilitating this learning.

5/Being Friends

Let's tour the nursery school together. Spring is in the air, and as we explore the playground, we are confronted with a busy scene of sound and movement – children chasing one another, climbing ropes, shouting across the yard, dancing to music, swinging and sliding. As we stroll into the schoolroom, we see children feeding goldfish, finger-painting, playing house, pushing trains along the floor while making loud whistle noises. Some children stay at one activity for a long time; others switch frequently. Still others roam around the room, casually surveying what their classmates are doing.

To a new observer, these patterns of activity are what is most salient about the school. After we have watched for a while, however, we realize that more is going on. The activities we see are being produced by well-defined pairs and groups of three-and-a-half- and four-year-old children, and each pair or group is interacting in its own distinctive way. This distinctiveness becomes clear as we approach particular pairs more closely, watching their comings and goings and listening in on their conversations. When we do this, we find that we are no longer paying attention simply to sounds and movements and games, but that we have become privy to the inner workings of friendships – friendships that have their own unique histories and cultures, satisfactions and tensions. By watching and listening carefully, keeping our focus on one pair at a time, we can gain some glimmerings of insight into the enterprise of being friends.

We begin by focusing our attention on a boy and a girl, both blond and blue-eyed:

Gregory is sitting by himself on the long two-person swing, while Amy is some distance away, using a hose to fill a pail of water.

'Beep, beep, I'm on the airplane,' Gregory says, not very loudly, not obviously directed at anyone but himself. But his meaning is clear enough to Amy, who comes right over, carrying two pails full of muddy water. Gregory looks at the pails, shakes his head disapprovingly, and exclaims, 'No, no!' Amy looks slightly chagrined. She dutifully returns to the sandbox, gets two different pails, brings them back, and places them on the 'airplane', which she then boards herself. This time Gregory seems to approve.

Soon after, Amy leaves the plane again. I ask Gregory where she has gone and he explains, in a knowing tone that suggests the answer is obvious, that Amy had to go take off her apron.

Before Amy returns, Kevin – the largest boy in the class – comes over and gets on what he believes to be a swing, but what Gregory, Amy, and we all know is actually a plane. Anxiety flickers over Gregory's face and there is a tremor in his voice. But he speaks up clearly. 'No! That's Amy's place.'

Kevin doesn't budge, however. Amy returns – apronless – and confronts him more directly: 'Get off! Get off!' Kevin finally ambles off, leaving Amy and Gregory by themselves. They fly on the plane together, facing out in opposite directions as they slowly glide back and forth, at the same time conducting an intense, quiet conversation. They are speaking so softly that we can't make out any of the words, except that each of their parts in the dialogue is frequently punctuated with the word, 'Remember?' in apparent references to experiences they have shared in the past.

By now we have seen enough to know that Gregory and Amy are not casual acquaintances who happened to board a plane together. They are intimate friends who, I discover, live next door to one another and have known each other for most of their lives. More clearly than any of the other pairs of friends in the class, Gregory and Amy have a strong attachment – a relationship that provides a basic sense of belongingness. Gregory and Amy have secure attachments to their parents as well, and each of them is able to interact with other children. Nevertheless, each seems to derive an important part of their identity from the other.

Now we turn to another part of the playground:

After Kevin's brief occupation of Gregory and Amy's airplane, he runs over to the wagons, takes one, and then calls out in a deep, musical voice, in the manner of a rallying cry, 'Mambadooly-la-ay!' In a distant corner of the yard, a smaller boy looks up alertly, pauses for a moment, and then shouts back, in a thinner voice but the same tone and cadence, 'Mambadooly-la-ay!' Then the small boy, Jake, runs over to the wagons and takes one too. Kevin and Jake glance at each other, smile briefly, and then – without further words – plunge into a frenzied round of activity. They race around the yard together, pulling their wagons and making blaring truck noises. They take turns pulling each other, running as fast as they can and screeching. A teacher looks over with a 'not again!' look of apprehension that is only partially feigned, since it seems inevitable that the wagon will topple over at any moment. To her relief, Kevin and Jake abandon the wagons and go indoors to finger-paint, getting their hands paint-soaked in the process. At some imperceptible signal from one or the other they suddenly leave the painting table and run into the bathroom. We don't look in, but we can't avoid hearing their proud shouts, 'Making yukkie!' When we next notice Kevin and Jake, they are in the 'house' area, lying in bed together and laughing hysterically.

Kevin's and Jake's friendship has a history, too, but it extends back only as far as the third or fourth week of the school year. At that time Kevin, who had arrived in the United States only months before from his native country, Africa, and Jake, a red-haired, freckle-faced American, discovered that they had very similar styles and tempos of play, styles that emphasized sound and motion, with relatively little conversational exchange. If the defining quality of Gregory's and Amy's friendship is attachment, that of Kevin's and Jake's is camaraderie.

Once more I look up, survey the larger scene of activity – storytelling in one corner, puppet play in another – and then concentrate my attention upon another pair of children. Tony and David are both wearing firemen's helmets and are absorbed in roles that I later learn are patterned after characters in a television series called *Emergency*. Some people at first take Tony and David for brothers because they have the same straight dark hair, olive complexions, and finely chiselled features, as well as the same unusually high degree of verbal facility and capacity for fantasy. If Tony and David were brothers, Tony would be the older brother and David the younger. In fact, they are only six months apart in age. But Tony is several inches taller and the acknowledged authority in all matters of fact or procedure. David will frequently propose new ideas to be incorporated into their fantasy world to Tony, who then has the final say about whether or not to adopt them. In the game of 'Emergency', Tony is the chief, David the deputy. While we observe, Tony and David address some of their comments to us as well as to one another.

> (David runs purposefully to another part of the yard, finds a puddle, and reports back to Tony.)
> *David*: Hey, chief – there's some water back here. There's water here!
> (Tony comes over and assesses the situation. He speaks authoritatively.)
> *Tony*: David, let's test the water. Let's get some stuff in that water.
> (The two become busily engaged in shovelling sand into the puddle. I ask them to explain just what they are doing.)
> *Tony*: We're feeding our . . .
> *David* (eagerly breaking in): Fish.
> *Tony* (overruling him): Whales.
> *David*: We're men. We take care of whales.
> (I ask them why firemen are feeding whales.)
> *Tony*: We're firemen and that's why.
> *David*: They also take care of whales.
> *Tony*: We're in our fire station and we're the good guys and they're bad guys.
> *David*: He's the chief. The chief is directing everything. And also they have walkie-talkies. (David looks at Tony for confirmation of his last statement.)
> *Tony*: They sometimes do, they sometimes don't.

The roles of chief and deputy provide an apt characterization of Tony's and David's friendship. In addition to 'Emergency', Tony and David play 'Star Wars' and house, do artwork, and read books together. Tony is invariably the mentor, pointing things out to David, instructing him, and guiding his activity, and David is his generally attentive student. The foundation for these roles was laid before Tony and David arrived at this nursery school – they had been friends at a previous school, beginning when they were not yet three years old. The mentor and student roles were reinforced in the new nursery school, however. Tony has been attending the school since the fall, while David did not transfer from their previous school until the winter. When David arrived, Tony took him under his wing, systematically showing him around the school and formally introducing him to other children. Tony also provided a model of conduct for David, imparting elements both of his own character and of the school's social order. For example:

> David notices Ricky and Caleb doing something that he finds objectionable. He pulls out a plastic gun and shoots them, shouting 'Don't do that!' Tony watches the scene and seems disturbed. He turns to David and tells him, in an admonitory tone, 'David – no shooting in school.' Then Tony goes off by himself to have juice. Moments later, Ricky and Caleb start shooting. David turns to them and says, in a slightly more strident tone than Tony's, 'No shooting in school!'

David acknowledges Tony's greater expertise in the ways of the school and of the world, and frequently asks him for advice or assistance. Tony, for his part, seems fully aware of his influence on David. On one occasion, after David has told me that he likes Jake, I ask Tony why he thinks this is the case. Tony thinks for a moment and then replies, 'I think he likes him because I played with him.' From Tony's point of view, David would be unlikely to acquire any important new attitudes in school without his own involvement. In most cases, this appraisal would probably be correct.

Our observations in the nursery school should serve to make us realize that there is no single underlying basis for children's friendships. The friendships of pre-school children – like those of older children and of adults – have many different functions. Friends are security givers, standards against whom one can measure oneself, partners in activities that cannot be engaged in alone, guides to unfamiliar places, and apprentices who confirm one's own developing sense of competence and expertise. Some friendships seem to be based most importantly in one or another of these functions. Thus Gregory's and Amy's friendship may remind us most clearly of the attachment between adult spouses, Kevin's and Jake's friendship of the camaraderie between fellow workers, Tony's and David's friendship of the complementary relationship between teachers and their students. In each of these cases, however, it is possible to discern a multiplicity of functions – acceptance, belongingness, companionship, and other provisions all coming together in a single relationship. Although we cannot always be sure of the precise mix of rewards that is being provided in a particular friendship, it is evident that these relationships have tremendous value for the children involved.[1]

Because of the many functions served by children's friendships, it is impossible to predict with any degree of certainty which pairs or groups of children will become friends. If there is a single predictive principle, however, it is that children are most likely to be attracted to those who are similar to themselves. Dozens of studies have documented the tendency for pairs of friends to be of approximately the same age, the same sex, the same size, the same level of intelligence, and the same degree of physical maturity.[2] Many of the observed similarities between friends can be explained in part by the fact that children can make friends only with others with whom they have an opportunity to interact. Prevailing patterns of residential arrangement and school assignment dictate that these opportunities will be restricted in large measure to children who share demographic and socio-economic backgrounds, as well as the values and attitudes that are associated with these backgrounds.

Within a particular neighbourhood or classroom, however, there is further 'filtering', so that those pairs who become friends – and who stay friends for at least some period of time – are especially likely to have similar activity styles, interests, and values. These resemblances breed friendship because they encourage interaction and facilitate social comparison. Moreover, the discovery that one resembles another child in a previously unknown way is sometimes the occasion for jubilation, because it demonstrates that one is not alone in one's tastes and views. For young children, even the discovery that both like bananas or have pink curtains in their rooms can produce great excitement. For older children, the discoveries are more likely to involve social and cultural attitudes: 'You like the Psychotic Pumpkin? That's incredible – I've got all their records!' In such ways the recognition of similarities can contribute to the growth of self-acceptance.

Children's friendships may also be facilitated by the discovery that they share attitudes towards other members of their peer group. While walking home from school with Eileen, a newcomer to her school, twelve-year-old Naomi discovered that the two of them had very similar views of their classmates. This discovery rapidly led to a close friendship:

I'm really becoming good friends with Eileen. She feels a lot of the things I feel. We both like the other people in the 'club' [Naomi's old set of girlfriends] but feel that they're really immature and kissassish about the boys. I really like all of them but sometimes I need friendship at a higher level – namely Eileen. She feels just like I do about the boys – all ego, no sensitivity. Except for Brad, who's nice but young. At Felicia's party I was get-

ting really fed up with the spin-the-bottle games and
how immature everyone was. So I left the room, took
the phone in the hall and called Eileen. It was really
nice.[3]

It is fair to say that every friendship must be built at
least in part on a base of similarity, but there is more to
it than that. Most friendships also depend on comple-
mentarity – a fit between two people in which each brings
something distinctive to the relationship and in which, as
a result, each can learn something from the other. A wild,
adventurous boy forms an alliance with a gentler soul who
serves as a steadying influence. A girl with quiet charm
becomes friends with a more outgoing girl who lacks social
graces. There is reason to believe that, as children grow
older, they become increasingly able to tolerate and appreciate differences between themselves and their friends.[4]
But complementary exchanges can in fact be found in
friendships at all ages: As Robert White notes, 'Each member can supply the other with something he lacks, at the
same time serving as a model from whom the desirable
quality can be copied.'[5] It is not too much to suggest that
such complementary relationships between friends play a
central role in the process of psychological development.

As children grow older, they tend to become more concerned with defining clearly just who is – and who is not
– a 'friend' or a 'best friend'. 'When I asked a boy [of eleven
or twelve] who his best friends were,' social psychologist
Gary Fine reports, 'he often made a big production of the
answer, thinking very carefully, and then explaining why
his best friends should be ranked in that particular order.'[6]
Children use many criteria for deciding whether another
person is a friend, and these criteria change over the course
of childhood. Thus, whereas a pre-schooler may regard
as a best friend someone he plays with a great deal of the
time, a pre-adolescent may be more likely to label as a best

friend someone who will stick up for him – and whom he will stick up for – in times of need.[7]

A particularly important criterion of friendship, among children as well as adults, is the sharing of personal information – 'private' facts and feelings that are not known to other people.[8] This aspect of a close friendship is eloquently captured in Charlotte Zolotow's book for children, *My Friend John*:

> I know everything about John and he knows everything about me. We know where the secret places are in each other's house, and that my mother cooks better but his father tells funnier jokes ... We always stick together because I'm good at fights, but John's the only one besides my family who knows that I sleep with my light on at night. He can jump from the high diving board but I know he's afraid of cats ... He saw me cry once and the day he broke his arm I ran home and got his mother for him. We know what's in each other's refrigerator, which steps creak on each other's stairs and how to get into each other's house if the door is locked. I know who he really likes and he knows about Mary too. John is my best friend and I'm his.[9]

Because close friends already know so much about each other, their fears and failings as well as their strengths, friendships can give children a unique opportunity to relate to another person openly and without self-consciousness. 'A friend is a person with whom I may be sincere,' Ralph Waldo Emerson wrote. 'Before him I may think aloud.'

The sharing of personal facts and feelings also relates to some of the obligations of friendship. Among older children, friends may be expected to reveal their innermost feelings to one another, and any failure to do so may be viewed as a violation of the basic terms of the friendship. 'The worst thing is that she didn't tell me,' one twelve-year-old lamented to her teacher. 'For all our "open relationship" she told three other people she was angry – and not me!' Perhaps an even more serious violation of friendship among older children is the betrayal of a secret. In one recent study, older children expressed doubts about the future survival of a friendship in which one child had 'blabbed' about his friend to someone else. 'If you can't trust your best friend,' one thirteen-year-old remarked, 'who *can* you trust?'[10] Being friends involves responsibilities as well as rewards.

Like adults' closest friendships and loves, children's friendships rarely contain only positive sentiments. Because they involve such extensive contact and interdependence, close friendships invariably give rise to negative feelings as well. Young children, who do not yet understand that one can regard someone both positively and negatively at the same time, are likely to deal with negative feelings by deciding – for the moment – that they aren't friends any more. Even Amy, whose attachment to Gregory was strong and enduring, would sometimes solemnly announce, 'I'm not Gregory's friend,' usually after she had observed him playing with someone else. As children grow older, they are likely to come to a fuller, even if sometimes more painful, appreciation of their mixed feelings towards their closest friends. From an eleven-year-old girl:

What a wrong day! Lindsey is getting me more and more irritated every day. I think we're both beginning a *bad* relationship. She bothers me a lot. We kind of made a commitment to tell each other everything. But no, she had just recently started to tell me things, about her and Alan, and that she hated me during the summer. I wonder if she still does hate me, maybe . . . I always have to listen to how she feels but she won't listen to how I feel. I hate her as of the present moment, but I will never take off the bead ring I have that she gave me. I love her

alot and never want to part as a friend, but there are
times I just can't stand when she does things like this.

Despite the rewards that close friends provide for one
another, conflicts are unavoidable. Among pre-school
children, pairs of friends who spend much of their time
together will almost inevitably devote some of this time to
quarrelling.[11] Among older children, although friends may
be expected to be constantly loyal and supportive, to
respect each other's rights and needs, and to agree on just
about everything, such expectations cannot be fulfilled in
reality. In some cases, the conflicts that arise prove to be
irreconcilable and lead to the ending of a friendship. In
other cases, children are able to work through their disagreements in constructive ways. As one boy concluded,
'I think fights are an important part of a close friendship.
Nobody is perfect, and you're bound to get a close friend
angry at you once in a while. If you don't work it out things
build up and pretty soon the whole relationship is blown.
In fact sometimes if you have a real fight and find out
you're still friends, then you've got something that is
stronger.'[12]

Clearly, not everything about being friends is 'good' for
the child. The vicissitudes of friendship may sometimes
produce disappointment and anguish. And the strong
influence that close friends have on one another may sometimes seem harmful. In the nursery school class that we
observed, for example, the teachers sometimes feared that
Gregory's and Amy's attachment was leading to over-
dependence, and that Kevin's and Jake's camaraderie was
limiting their range of activities and reinforcing 'holy
terrorism'. There are times, especially with somewhat
older children, when parents or teachers conclude that a
close friendship is doing so much harm that they must try
to end it; in at least some cases, such a course of action
may be justified. In the large majority of cases, however,

I am convinced that the rewards of children's close friendships outweigh their liabilities. The friendships of Gregory and Amy, Kevin and Jake, Tony and David may last for a lifetime; or they may fade during the coming summer. For the time being, though, they are examples of the wondrous state of being friends – human relationships of remarkable strength, satisfaction, and importance.

6/Losing Friends

Janey it's lonely all day long since you moved away. When I walk in the rain and the leaves are wet and clinging to the sidewalk I remember how we used to walk home from school together ... I remember how we'd go home for dinner and I could hardly wait for dinner to end to call you. But sometimes you called me first ... I didn't want you to move away. You didn't want to either. Janey maybe some day we'll grow up and live near each other again.[1]

Friendships end. They end in different ways, sometimes against the children's will, when one of them must move to a new city or school, and sometimes as a result of one or both children's own decision that the friendship is no longer viable. To these endings children have widely ranging reactions, from relative equanimity to deep despair. In most cases, however, losing friends is a stressful experience for the child.

I recently revisited the pre-school children in Berkeley with whom I had been spending time a year ago. These children were now between four and a half and five and a half. On my visit I immediately noticed that Ricky, once the most outgoing and popular boy in the class, seemed unusually quiet and subdued. Although he was playing with other children, he was engaged in activities that were beneath his usual level of sophistication – for example, jumping repeatedly on a plank – and he seemed to be playing with a lack of real involvement. I asked him whether anything was the matter, and he shook his head no. When I returned to school the next day, though, Ricky came up to me and said sadly, 'Buddy Josh, Buddy Tony, Buddy David.' I asked Ricky why he was saying that. 'Those are my buddies,' he replied, 'I miss them.' Towards the end of the previous year, Ricky, Josh, Tony, and David had formed a close clique. (Tony had succeeded in 'introducing' his protégé David to Ricky and Josh and the four had become frequent companions.) They were among the most imaginative children in the class and would often build parking garages, rush to put out fires, or man a spaceship together. Two months before my visit, Josh, Tony, and David were transferred by their parents from the half-day nursery school to an all-day pre-school. This left only Ricky of the original group in the old school. Although he seemed to understand the situation and to be adapting to it, his sense of loss was unmistakable.

In the case of five-year-old Erik, the child's reaction to the loss of a friend was more extreme. Erik had been best friends with Peter for two and a half years at their daycare centre. Peter gradually came to be more interested in playing with a new boy, Curtis, who had joined the group. Their teacher, Margaret Stubbs, recalls:

Finally Peter formed a relationship with Curtis which excluded Erik. Erik at first reacted to the change by expressing sadness and rage. For a time, he was unable to participate effectively in school activities. He seemed to need to show off in front of the group, even though he had never before sought attention so directly. He overreacted to criticism, with prolonged fussing and arguing, whereas previously he had been reasonable in his acceptance of his own misbehaviour and pragmatic in serving out the accompanying punishment. He rigorously protested Peter's new exclusion of him, and for a long time continued to interrupt Peter's new friendship with his presence.[2]

Although the loss of friends was a painful experience for both Ricky and Erik, it was easier for Ricky to deal with the loss. Whereas he had lost several friends at once, none of them was his single 'best friend', and he had other friendships to fall back on. Moreover, Ricky understood that his friends had changed schools because of a decision their parents had made ('You see, Josh's mother works,' he explained to me), rather than because of any desire to reject him. Ricky gradually began to spend more time with other children in the class, including some he had previously had little interest in. At the same time, he discovered new activities that he enjoyed, such as playing the role of 'daddy' in family role-play with some of the girls in the class. Thus Ricky's loss of friends had the hidden benefit of making new sorts of social relationships and experiences available to him.

For Erik, the situation was more difficult. Erik had lost his best friend, one who had been his bosom buddy for half his life. And although Peter had not been callous or cruel in his rejection of Erik, it was still a clear case of abandonment. Even for a five-year-old, questions of 'Why doesn't he like me?' and its common sequel 'What's wrong with me?' are likely to arise. Erik's displays of sadness, hostility, and attention seeking can be understood as reactions both to his sense of loss and to his newly aroused feelings of doubt about his own worth. After some time had passed, however, Erik was able to turn the loss of his friendship into a positive experience. 'Over time, Peter's new friendship solidified,' Stubbs reports, 'and Erik showed his distress behaviour less frequently. Instead, he seemed to become more serious in his schoolwork, more involved in activities for their own sake. Instead of showing off in front of the group, Erik became a group leader and a genuine helper to his peers. For the rest of the year, he never formed as close a friendship with another child in the class as he had had with Peter. But instead, he seemed to invest his energy quite successfully into developing his intellectual capacities and broadening his social network.'

As the stories of Ricky and Erik suggest, children's reactions to the endings of friendship vary greatly from case to case. When they move to a new school or neighbourhood, some children will feel intense pain while others will regard the move as an exciting, even if somewhat frightening, opportunity. Similarly, when he is rejected by a friend, one child will react by going into a prolonged depression, a second will do everything he can to win the friend back, and a third will immediately try to find a new friend as a replacement. Predicting the way in which a particular child will react to a particular breakup is by no means an easy matter. And social scientists, who have long been concerned with the effects of children's short-term and long-term separations from their parents, have done little systematic research on children's separations from their friends.

There is no shortage of speculation, however, about the effects of separation from friends. Much of this speculation has concerned the effects of moving, and most of it has been highly cautionary. Writing about the early school years, Harry Stack Sullivan declared that frequent moves often prove to be 'disastrous' influences on children's lives, and that any moves during this period may cause serious social handicaps.[3] More recently, a noted child psychologist has suggested that moving is likely to be traumatic both for pre-schoolers and for teenagers, whose 'lives are shattered by leaving their home towns and their home-town friends'.[4]

Severe reactions to moving may be understood in part as grief reactions to the loss of particularly close friends, people on whom one has come to depend for companionship and support. Feelings of loneliness, depression, irritability, and anger are all common responses to such loss. These feelings can be experienced by the child whose friend has moved away, just as they can by the child who has moved away herself. In at least some cases, like that of twelve-year-old Andrea, the pain can be intense:

> I've done so much thinking I have to write. I've said so much to myself and now it's got to come out. Sometimes I want to kill myself. Do I? Seriously, I've thought about it. My problem is that I want to go back to my old school and my real home.[5]

An additional difficulty is that the child who moves must now become integrated into a new social setting – where, to make matters worse, 'everyone acts as though they've known everyone for a long time'. For children of all ages, such moves can resurrect all of the difficulties and anxieties of the first arrival into a pre-school setting that I discussed in Chapter 4. Making new friends may sometimes be especially difficult for older children, since by the later childhood years cliques are likely to be well-established and difficult to penetrate.

After a move, the opportunity to keep in touch with old friends may be rewarding, but such contacts may also remind the child of how much she misses them. A thirteen-year-old who was transferred by her parents, with her own partial acquiescence, from one private school to another reported on an encounter she had with an old friend:

> I really miss Bancroft so much sometimes. At lunch I saw a really close friend – at least he was last year – and he was so nice. I felt like just leaving school and going to talk to him for the rest of the day. It just makes me feel so sad each time I talk to or see someone from there. I get so sad about not being there but at the same time

I'm so glad I'm not. It's confusing and it hurts like hell.

Such ambivalence may be characteristic of children who have moved from one setting to another, as they attempt to cope both with their feelings of loss and their need to make the best of a new situation.

In addition to the immediate effects of having to leave old friends and make new ones, some writers have suggested that frequent moves are likely to have more lasting effects. In his book about mobility in the United States, *A Nation of Strangers*, Vance Packard reports on the prototypical case of a young man raised in a military family who had, since his boyhood, great difficulty in making close friendships: 'He was certain it was because his close friends when he was growing up were inevitably from military families and they were usually rotated out every two years. The pain of losing friends repeatedly caused him unwittingly, he suspected, to start shunning close friendships.'[6]

It must be emphasized that moving does not always have such severely negative effects on children. Children are likely to miss their old friends, to be sure, and often continue to think and talk about them for a long time. Young children sometimes incorporate their old friends into their fantasy play ('That's Ronny's space ship and this is mine') as a way of adjusting to the loss.[7] In many instances, children also make efforts to keep up their old ties through letters, phone calls, and occasional visits. Some older children manage to maintain friendships for many years through such long-distance contacts. At the same time, many children look on their move as a positive opportunity, and most succeed in gradually making friends in their new locale. Although children's reactions to separations differ widely from case to case, I think that in general we can credit our children with a good deal of resilience. Parents and teachers should appreciate, however, that being forced to separate from one's friends and to enter a new social world is going to be stressful for children of any age, just as it is for adults. These are times when secure and supportive family relationships are especially important for the child.

Perhaps even more frequent than the separations that result from moving are the breakups that children themselves precipitate. Children's relationships are rarely disrupted permanently by a single dispute. Rather, the breakups are likely to be the final result of a gradual drifting apart, set in motion by one or both friends' increasing recognition that they no longer provide the same satisfactions to one another. As individual children grow up, their changing needs, abilities, and interests almost inevitably result in changing friendships. These changes are particularly striking as friends progress, each at his own rate and in his own way, from childhood to adolescence. 'Sometimes a kid grows up and sometimes the friend doesn't,' an older child explains. 'So then all of a sudden you find out you don't have anything in common. You like boys and she's still interested in dolls.'[8] In an account of four boys who were studied throughout their childhood and adolescent years, as part of a longitudinal study launched in the 1930s, Mary Cover Jones provides an extended description of such changes:

The four boys started out as close friends in elementary school. At the time, they were 10–10½ years old, with only four months difference between them in age. They were all above average in ability, with only 10 points difference in IQ. They were healthy, lively youngsters from good homes, doing well in school, and enjoying life in general. So firm were their bonds that even though they were separated in junior high school classrooms, they continued to mention each other as friends until the eighth grade.

Then came separations which appeared to result from differences in social maturity and in rate of physical development. Bob, the most advanced in skeletal build, was also socially most mature. For example, when observed at a dance for sixteen-year-olds, Bob was described as 'poised, unselfconscious, competent in steering his partners around the floor, adultly incon-spicuous'. Bob pulled ahead of the group at this time in social status and remained at the top in this respect. How were the other boys affected? What adjustments did they make in the high school years?

One, Nelson, became a runner-up – something of a 'fringe member' of Bob's prestige group, although they continued to be best friends throughout the school years. Nelson was slightly below average in physical maturity during this period and less sure of himself in social situ-ations. At the high school dance, for example, Nelson danced in a strangely crab-like fashion, holding his partner at almost a right angle to himself. However, by dint of greater effort, which our observers often noted, he was able to keep up with Bob and to be included in his crowd.

Harry, the least physically mature of the clique, but as interested as Bob and Nelson in social activities, was not able to meet the social requirements of mixed-sex group situations with the same maturity as Bob or Nelson. At the school dance, Harry, chewing gum, look-ing somewhat bravely worried, traded dances with other boys as the younger crowd usually do. His inexperience made him overly eager to conform to the accepted rituals; he covered up pauses in conversations by nervous giggles and 'kiddish' tricks like shadow-boxing. He was dropped by his erstwhile friends, had a short period of disappointment over this rejection, but soon found an equally immature companion with whom he was happy. In fact, he probably functioned more easily in this new situation than his old friend, Nelson, who just managed to make the higher status group and had to work to stay there.

The last of the original four friends is Phil, whose physical development was slightly advanced and could have been a social asset. But Phil was not psychologically ready for the mixed group activities of his agemates. He selected as a friend a new boy who, like himself, might be described as relatively asocial. At a party in the eighth grade, 'when the girls insisted upon dancing, Phil fled to the office and practiced typing, returning later to play a game of chess with his friend, Pierce'.[9]

Jones's chronicle emphasizes the close interplay of physical and psychological changes, on the one hand, and changes in friendship, on the other. Her account helps to make clear that the endings of friendships and their replacement with new ones should usually be taken as signs of normal development rather than of social inadequacy. As Benjamin Spock writes, 'The very fact that friendships wax and wane is evidence that at each phase of growth children are apt to need something different from their friends and, therefore, have to find a new one from time to time.'[10]

But although such endings are normal and necessary aspects of development, children often have great difficulty in dealing with such breakups. As with the endings of marriages and love affairs, the endings of friendships are seldom completely mutual. One child typically becomes disenchanted with the relationship sooner than the other and becomes the 'breaker-upper'. This is highlighted in the following account of a breakup as reconstructed by Myron Brenton:

At the start of the third grade, eight-year-old Susie was ecstatic about her new friend Carla. The two girls took to each other immediately, and were soon constant companions – giggling, gossiping, playing and doing homework together.

Then, halfway into the school year, a new girl came into the class. Tamara, just arrived from Hawaii, was exotic with her beautiful eyes, black hair and golden skin. Carla thought she was super. Very quickly these two saw each other all the time, and Susie was left out. Every time she asked Carla to come over, the answer was, 'I'm busy.' One day, cruelly, Carla said, 'Tamara's a lot more fun than you.'[11]

In a breakup of this sort, not only the rejected child but also the rejecter is likely to suffer. In the wake of her cruelty to Susie, Carla may experience considerable guilt. This guilt can serve a useful function, if it leads Carla towards greater sensitivity towards the feelings of others. As children grow older, they typically develop such sensitivity, and the decision to end a friendship that one has outgrown may become an agonizing one. Twelve-year-old Naomi was faced with such difficulties as she contemplated her friendship with Marcy:

She's such a phoney, cutesy, show off, hypocrite. But I can't tell her that she bugs me, or why, because she gets defensive, confused, and hurt. I've tried, because we have a pact to tell each other our gripes instead of whisper to each other about them. But Marcy thinks I'm her friend, and I can't not be friends with her. Lately I haven't wanted to be around her.

Handling such a conflict sensitively is a difficult test for the child's developing social skills. In many such cases, the best resolution – which was, in fact, accomplished by Naomi – is to continue the friendship, but at a lower level of intensity.

Coming to terms with rejection by a friend is even more

difficult. For younger children, such as five-year-old Erik, the discovery that one's friend no longer wants to play with one may be incomprehensible and, hence, particularly hurtful. And even if the child can understand, in abstract terms, that he and his friend no longer have as much in common as they used to, the rejection is still likely to come as a devastating blow.

Especially as they approach adolescence, children sometimes become intensely preoccupied with the status of their friendships, as if to prepare themselves for the endings that may take place. In a class of eleven-, twelve-, and thirteen-year-olds taught by Peggy Stubbs, some of the younger girls who were maturing more quickly sought to establish friendships with the other girls. As a result, others of the younger girls became acutely aware of the possibility of rejection. One of them, Sarah, wrote poignantly to her teachers:

> Rachel is spending all her time with Paula Davis and deserting me. Rachel is conversing very loudly with two idiots in her cubby and I can't concentrate. Rachel is changing, she is not Rachel any more.

Rachel herself was upset by the same changing situation, although her perception of it differed somewhat from Sarah's:

> Oh, I feel so horrible about friends. Everybody is deserting their best friend and everybody hates someone else and Paula Davis has been stranded with nobody – except me and Sarah, and Christine has run off with Liz and Joan has moved up from being an eleven-year-old to a twelve or thirteen-year-old and, oh well, I suppose it happens every year.

Although these girls were distressed by the changes in friendships that seemed to be taking place, their sensitivity to the fluctuations is likely to prove valuable in the long run. Such sensitivity can help children to identify accurately the emerging differences that may lead to endings, rather than hastily blaming these endings on other children's malice or on their own basic inadequacies. These assessments of the causes of a breakup play a critical role in determining one's reactions to it. Whereas self-blame, for example, may discourage children from attempting to form new friendships (on the ground that 'no one could ever like me'), a fuller understanding of the psychological differences that led to a breakup can help them to establish more satisfactory friendships in the future. There is reason to think, incidentally, that girls are more sensitive to the vicissitudes of relationships than boys are, for reasons that I will consider in the next chapter. And it may be in part for this reason that women seem to handle separation and loss more effectively than men in adulthood as well.[12]

Children may also find it easier to deal with a rejection if they have already had some practice in breaking up. One of the functions of children's games and rituals of friendship may be to provide this sort of practice. In their survey of such rituals throughout Great Britain, Iona and Peter Opie conclude that 'the finger of friendship is the little finger'. For example:

They link the little fingers of their right hands and shake them up and down, declaring:

Make friends, make friends,
Never, never break friends.

They quarrel, and their friendship is ended with the formula,

Break friends, break friends,
Never, never make friends,

repeated in a like manner, but, in Croydon, with the little fingers moistened, and in Portsmouth with linked thumbs. They make up again, intoning,

We're broken before,
We break now –
and they separate their little fingers,
We'll never break any more,
and they intertwine their little fingers again, squeezing
tightly (Weston-super-Mare). Alternatively, in places as
far apart as South Molton and Cleethorpes (and commonly in the London area), they say,
Make up, make up, never row again,
If we do we'll get the cane,
and thereupon they slap hands or smack each other. In
Radnorshire they hook little fingers, touch thumbs, and
then turn hands over and clap.[13]

When children use rituals like these, of course, they are
playing at making and breaking friends. In addition to their
entertainment value, such rituals probably help children
to work through their disputes and, at the same time,
prepare them for the real breakups that ultimately occur.

No amount of preparation or practice makes a rejection
easy to handle, however. More generally, the ending of a
close friendship, whether because of physical separation or
psychological disengagement, usually represents a crisis of
some proportion in the child's life. Parents often seem to
underestimate the importance of these losses, especially
when they are dealing with younger children. They tend
to downplay the loss, assuring the child, 'Don't worry,
you'll find another friend,' thus revealing the misconcep-
tion that young friends are like standardized, replaceable
parts. Parents would do better to take the situation more
seriously. 'Talk about the feelings and emotions involved,'
Myron Brenton advises. '[Convey to your child] that you
understand how hard it can be to lose a friend, that under
the circumstances feeling sad, angry, hurt or rejected is
perfectly normal, that the friendship had some good things
and some bad things to it and that neither aspect should

be overlooked ... Children should be helped to realize that in time they'll find other friends – but they mustn't expect a new friend to "replace" a former one.'[14]

These goals are not always easy to achieve, but they seem worth striving for. In helping children to deal with the loss of friends, parents and teachers may also find children's books to be useful resources.[15] Separation from friends is a frequent theme of books for both young and older children, and many of them show keen insight into the children's feelings and concerns. There may also be some children who are continually losing friends, either as rejecters of others or as those who perpetually seem to be dropped themselves. Patterns such as these may be signs of deeper problems, and in such instances professional help may be useful.

For most children, losing friends is a normal and necessary part of growing up. The distress that such losses are likely to produce should not be underestimated. In most cases, however, children are eventually able to turn these losses into gains – experiences that channel their interests and social networks in productive and satisfying ways.

7/Boys, Girls, and Groups

During the first two years of life, when infants and toddlers interact at all, they do so in twosomes – almost never in groups of three or more. At this age, children's groups provide many opportunities for pair interaction, but they do not seem to function as collective entities. Before the age of two, moreover, there is little evidence of sex preferences in children's play. When given the opportunity to do so, boys seem as interested in playing with girls as with other boys, and girls show a similar lack of prejudice. By the time children are three and four years old, however, there are changes both in the size of their groups and in their sexual composition. Although nursery school children still spend much of their time in pairs, they begin to play in larger groups as well and to become concerned with group belonging. At the same time, children become more likely to prefer others of their own sex as playmates and friends. These developments continue into later childhood. By the time children are eleven or twelve years old, groups have come to assume major importance and the sex segregation of these groups is almost total. These interrelated themes – the growing role of groups in children's lives and the cleavage between boys and girls that characterizes groups – will be my concerns in this chapter.

A group, whether it is an informal clique, a gang, a club, or a team, is a social entity which transcends the level of individual personalities and two-person relationships.[1]

Belonging to a group can provide the child with a variety of resources that an individual friendship often cannot – a sense of collective participation, experience with organizational roles, and group support in the enterprise of growing up. Groups also pose for the child some of the most acute problems of social life – of inclusion and exclusion, conformity and independence. As we will see, groups may also come to serve somewhat different functions for the two sexes, especially as children approach adolescence. Boys seem most likely to emphasize the solidarity of the group, while girls seem to view the group more as a network of intimate friendships.

The Israeli kibbutz provides a unique illustration of how a strong sense of group belonging can develop early in life. In two kibbutzim studied by Helen Faigin,[2] the children spend several hours each day with their parents and the rest of the day and night with a group of about six children of the same age. Each group lives in a children's house, under the supervision of a caretaker. By the age of two, the children have already come to refer consistently to the group as 'we' and to all property and activities connected with the group as 'ours'. (In contrast, anything the child has or does in his parents' private room is 'mine'.) The toddlers are highly aware of the group's membership, so that whenever a child is away from the group the absence is invariably noticed and mentioned. The children also develop a strong sense of group loyalty and pride. If a child is hit or teased by a child from an older or younger group, others in the child's own group immediately rise to his defence. And kibbutz children brag to outsiders about their group, often in invidious terms: 'We have a nice house and you don't' or 'We went for a walk and you didn't'. In these two- and three-year-olds, we can observe the genesis of the same sort of group identification that plays so prominent a role in adult social life.

For children reared in a noncommunal environment,

group identification typically comes later and in a less
dramatic form. For three- and four-year-olds in American
nursery schools, however, group membership is likely to
take on considerable importance. 'Our' class and 'their'
class, 'our' team and 'their' team soon become well-learned
and significant distinctions. By the age of three or four,
children also begin to take specific roles within groups.
Over a period of several months, for example, Josh, Tony,
and Caleb served together as a crew of a spaceship docked
in their nursery school playground. Their assignments
were patterned after the roles of the crew on the television
show *Star Trek*. Josh, the leader of the band, was Captain
Kirk and made the major decisions. Tony, the most verbally
facile, was Spock and in charge of preparing the countdown
lists. Caleb, the smallest and most obliging, was Scotty and
followed the others' lead. Children's roles in groups are
usually less fixed and formal, however. When playing
house, for example, Molly may sometimes be a 'mother',
sometimes a 'baby', and sometimes even a 'kitty'. Such
group play provides children with experience in dealing
with the multiple and shifting roles that characterize social
life.

In the early school years children often become especially
interested in forming 'official' groups. A commonly observed pattern is for a group of eight- or nine-year-olds
to form a club – typically admitting only boys or only girls
– invest a tremendous amount of energy into deciding on
officers and their official titles, find nothing to do after that,
and then disband.[3] For my own part, I was a charter
member of a club for seven-year-olds called the Penguins
whose two major activities were acquiring extensive information about penguins and standing outside in the freezing
weather without a coat for as long as we could. Like most
other groups of this sort, the Penguins did not last very
long. But in the making and unmaking of such groups,
children are conducting what may be informative experi-

ments in social organization. Through such experiences, children develop increasingly sophisticated understandings of groups, from an early conception of a group as merely a collection of people in one place to a later conception of a group as a collective organization in which individuals are united by common interests and goals.[4]

Children's groups characteristically take on their greatest importance in late childhood – the years between about nine and twelve. At a time when children must leave the safety of the family, to become more autonomous persons, a group of friends can play a valuable supportive role, especially in the domains of sexual and emotional development. Despite the psychoanalytic notion that childhood is a period of sexual latency – the calm before the storm of puberty – sexual concerns are likely to be prominently revealed in groups of nine- to twelve-year-olds. American boys, for example, are likely to participate in 'bull sessions' devoted to the exchange of sexual information. According to Gary Fine, 'These sessions are filled with loud (almost hysterical) giggly laughter, insults, and bravado,' all of which may testify to the underlying significance of the topics being discussed.[5] Although group discussions may arouse anxiety, they may also provide needed reassurance and support as children deal with the concerns of growing up.

At the same time, children's groups pose the central issue of inclusion and exclusion. Even among toddlers in the kibbutz, group membership is closely linked to the exclusion of nonmembers. On the kibbutz carousel, for example, the children always make room for members of their own group but do not let members of other groups join them. In nursery school, as we have seen in previous chapters, inclusion and exclusion are constant themes of social life. It is through the continuing negotiation of who is 'in' and who is 'out' that children establish and maintain group boundaries. When Josh, Tony, and Caleb want to play spaceship, they usually shout to one another and discourage any other children from joining in. A revealing exception comes on a day that Tony is absent from school and another boy, Eddie, is allowed on board:

> When I inquire into the matter, Josh (Captain Kirk) tells me that Eddie is Spock, adding that 'He's on my crew'.
>
> 'But I thought Tony was Spock,' I protest.
>
> Josh looks at me disdainfully and then explains the obvious: 'Tony's not here today.'
>
> 'Well, how about when Tony gets back?'
>
> Josh glances at Eddie and replies, 'Then *he's* not playing.'

Eddie was not admitted to regular membership in the space group because he had relatively little in common with Josh, Tony, and Caleb. Eddie was slower-moving and slower-talking than the other three boys and had trouble keeping up with their often frenetic pace. In addition, because of his shoulder-length hair, Eddie appeared 'girlish' to the other boys. These differences contributed to his exclusion from the space group. For if pairs of friends tend to be similar to one another, similarity of attributes and skills typically plays an even larger role in determining the membership of cliques and groups.[6]

The membership of a group may take shape in several different ways. Sometimes an individual child with valued skills plays a central role, with others entering the group by gaining the leader's approval. In other cases the group begins with an existing pair of friends, who then proceed to include others in their activities. Josh and Tony became friends early in the year and only later took Caleb, a slightly younger and smaller boy, into their group as a sort of junior member. In still other instances the group is based primarily on joint participation in a particular activity

Whether the activity is playing in a band or building sand-castles, children will be included only if they have the skills and interests that enable them to take part. All of these processes of group formation are likely to produce a relatively homogeneous membership. Just as in groups of adolescents and adults, moreover, there are strong pressures to exclude the 'deviant' child, whether the difference is with respect to appearance, skills, or temperament. In many school settings, race is another basis of group membership. 'They [other black girls] get mad because you've made a white friend,' a black twelve-year-old reports. 'They say that blacks are supposed to have black friends and whites are supposed to have white friends.'[7] Indeed, the link between group solidarity and similarity is so prevalent as to approach the status of a universal law of social behaviour.

Groups also have the effect of *making* their members – or prospective members – similar to one another. There is usually strong pressure on children to conform to the expectations and standards of their groups, both because of concern about being accepted and because of the assumption that 'if everyone in my group is doing it, it must be right'. The influence of group membership on children's behaviour is especially striking in the kibbutz. Even in the youngest kibbutz groups, the children themselves play an important role in enforcing standards of behaviour. When one of the children has a toileting accident, for example, the others all look at him and shout, 'Haggai did a BM, Haggai did a BM! Not on the floor, Haggai, not on the floor!' Similarly, when one child has hit another and made him cry, all the other group members come up and hit the first child. 'How many times do I have to tell you not to hit other children?' one of them adds. Such peer influence proves to be extremely effective in regulating the children's behaviour.

The degree to which children conform to group norms

and beliefs appears to increase during the years of child-hood, often reaching its peak at about the age of twelve.[8] In a famous study conducted thirty years ago, Muzafer Sherif and his colleagues observed the ways in which social norms were established and enforced among two groups of eleven- to twelve-year-old boys at a summer camp.[9] Each of the groups developed its own unique set of stan-dards. The boys in one cabin came to prize toughness. The norm apparently originated when a leader of the group injured his foot and did not tell anyone about it. From then on, 'Members were "he-men", bearing pain, rough and tough, turning the air blue with curses.'[10] Meanwhile, the other group of boys came to emphasize consideration, humility, good language, and prayer. Once established, these norms held almost complete sway over the boys' behaviour. Wayward members who did not do things 'right' found themselves receiving reprimands and silent treatment from their peers. Given these penalties, it did not take long for them to bring their behaviour back in line with the group standards.

The pressure to conform may sometimes be even greater for the child who is not already a member of a group but who wishes to become one. In such cases, the child may struggle almost desperately to behave in ways that will be acceptable to the group members. One twelve-year-old girl candidly sought advice in this endeavour from her teachers:

I was wondering if either of you could tell me about Marcy and her group, what they like and what they don't because I think they're my type more so than Mary Beth or Stephanie etc. And I would like to know what they're interested in so in talking to them I know what they hate. The reason for this is because I might say something that might turn them off so every time I see them they won't say 'There goes the fag that said so and so.'[11]

In the view of some observers of contemporary American society, the peer group in late childhood (as well as in adolescence) has become a tyrannical and destructive force. 'At least in the United States,' Urie Bronfenbrenner charges, 'the peer group tends to undermine adult socialization efforts and to encourage egocentrism, aggression, and antisocial behaviour.'[12] In line with this view, a large-scale survey of American eleven-year-olds found that those children who were most peer-oriented were also those who reported engaging most often in 'antisocial' activities (such as lying to grownups, smoking, and using bad language) and least often in 'socially desirable' activities (such as helping someone, talking about books, and building something).[13] As David Riesman has noted, moreover, peer groups in an other-directed society can have the unfortunate effect of repressing individual differences in tastes, values, and even emotions.

Whereas the peer group's potential for harm cannot be denied, we should not overstate it. The childhood peer group's influence is probably seriously destructive only in a small minority of cases. The standards enforced by pre-adolescent groups are less often antisocial than they are simply mystifying, as when a mother must contend with 'a daughter's sudden desperate need to have a charm bracelet, or with the experience of finding that different coloured socks on left and right feet are not her son's sleepy error but a "must"'.[14] While such conformity may sometimes be disturbing, we must recognize that, like it or not, groups exert a strong influence on behaviour and beliefs throughout our lives. As Patricia Minuchin has argued, a period of rather strict conformity to peers in late childhood may be a part of a normal and ultimately valuable growth pattern through which children gradually come to terms with the influence of groups. Through group membership, the child edges away from the sway of the family, comes to rely for a time on peer-group standards, and finally – in the ideal case – learns to strike an appropriate balance between personal autonomy and the demands of social life.

The link between group membership and similarity – and the associated exclusion of 'deviants' – is manifest most dramatically in the domain of gender. By nursery school age there is already a considerable degree of sex segregation in children's spontaneous activities. The cleavage between boys' groups and girls' groups seems to be universal, suggesting the possibility that the pattern is influenced by biological predispositions.[15] There is some supporting evidence for this view. Even before the age of three, when the concepts of 'boy' and 'girl' are not yet well-established, children have been found to get along better with unfamiliar children of the same sex than of the opposite sex.[16] There may well be a greater compatibility of behavioural styles among children of the same sex – boys for instance seem to have a greater proclivity for rough-and-tumble play. Although we cannot be certain about it, such sex differences may have a biological basis.[17]

Whatever the biological input may be, it is certain that cultural influences play a central role in shaping and maintaining the sex-segregated pattern. Even before children enter nursery school, parents are likely to seek out same-sex playmates for their toddlers and to encourage 'sex-appropriate' activities. Such early learning is likely to be reinforced in nursery school. It has been found, for example, that boys and girls are more likely to play separately in traditional nursery schools, whose teachers have conventional views about boys' and girls' activities, than in 'open schools', which try to avoid sex-typed expectations about interests and personalities.[18] In the traditional schools, we can assume, the pattern of sex segregation is strengthened because boys and girls are often steered to different sorts of activities – typically more active physical play for boys and more sedate activities like painting and doll play for girls. The currently prevailing view among behavioural scientists, then, is that children of the same sex tend to flock together primarily because they are directed by their culture to different sets of activities, interests, and behavioural styles and taught, even if unintentionally, that someone of the other sex is too 'different' to be accepted as a group member.

The differentness of the other sex quickly becomes salient to pre-schoolers:

(Jake and Danny are on the big swing together.)
Laura (running up, excited): Can I get on?
Jake (emphatically): No!
Danny (even more emphatically): No!!
Jake: We don't want you on here. We only want boys on here.
(After Laura leaves, I ask Jake why he said that.)
Jake: Because we like boys – we like to have boys. If Laura gets on here, I'll put fire in her eye.

Sally is swinging by herself, and talking about the birthday party she will have (she will be four). She looks at Dwayne and says, 'You can't go to my birthday.' Then she turns to me and explains, 'Because he doesn't have any dresses on.' I don't respond, and Sally elaborates, 'No boys are coming to my birthday. No!'

Since I know that Sally has a strong 'crush' on Ricky, I pose a question that I expect will lead Sally to qualify her statement: 'How about Ricky? Could he come?'

But Sally is unbending: 'No, he's a boy.'

These expressions of hostility towards the opposite sex reflect culturally instilled attitudes. They suggest that the seeds of the sexual antagonism that has prevailed throughout human history may be sown very early in life.

But if the pattern of sex segregation is largely learned, then it may be possible for it to be unlearned too. Lisa Serbin and her co-workers conducted an experiment in which teachers in two classes attempted to increase co-operative cross-sex play among four-year-olds.[19] When they saw a mixed-sex pair or group of children playing together cooperatively, the teachers were supposed to comment approvingly so that the whole class could hear, indicating the children's names and what they were doing. For example: 'I like the tower John and Kathy are building with the blocks.' Such comments were made approximately every five minutes, insofar as it was possible, during a two-week period. During this time it was found that the rate of cross-sex cooperative play increased dramatically in each of the two classes – from 5–6 per cent to 20–28 per cent of the children's time. What is more, the increase did not come at the expense of same-sex play. The children came to associate with opposite-sex children more, without associating with same-sex children less.

Cross-sex play among pre-schoolers should indeed be encouraged. Although many children may still choose to associate with same-sex peers – others who are 'like me' in gender – most of the time, we should strive to break down the culturally imposed barriers that effectively prevent many children from associating with the opposite sex at all. Such cross-sex play can expose boys and girls to a wider range of behavioural styles and activities, expand their pool of potential friends, and help to give them a fuller appreciation of the qualities that are in fact shared by the two sexes. Despite these potential advantages of cross-sex play, the barriers are not easy to break down. In the final phase of the Serbin study, the teachers' comments were discontinued and followup observations were made of the children's activities. Once the reinforcements were withdrawn, the amount of cross-sex play immediately declined to the same low level it had been at before the experiment began. It seems that to increase cross-sex association, more extensive encouragement may be required. To be really effective, these efforts probably cannot be restricted to the school setting. They must be supported by a change of attitudes about sex roles and cross-sex friendship in the home and in the larger society.

Meanwhile, there is a substantial degree of sex segregation in pre-school groups. In the early school years, as groups themselves become more important, the cleavage between the sexes becomes even more prevalent, and in late childhood it is likely to be complete. In an extensive recent study of the friendship networks of nine- to eleven-year-olds, for example, there were no boys in any of the girls' cliques and no girls in any of the boys' cliques.[20] There were some individual cross-sex friendships at each grade level, but such friends were not admitted into the children's cliques or groups. Even school seating patterns tend to be sexually segregated, and children may place considerable pressure on mavericks who seem to be breaking out of the pattern. Janet Ward Schofield provides an illustration from a classroom of twelve-year-olds:

The chairs in Mr Socker's room are arranged in the shape of a wide shallow U. As the first few kids come into the room, Harry says to John, who is starting to sit down in an empty section of the room along one side of the U, 'Don't sit there, that's where all the girls sit.' Harry and John sit elsewhere . . . The empty section fills up with girls. As a matter of fact, the boy–girl separation in the classroom today is complete with the girls occupying one side and most of the base of the U and the boys occupying the other side.[21]

During the later elementary school years, children also begin to show a 'romantic' interest in the opposite sex, paving the way for the full-fledged emergence of heterosexual interest in early adolescence. But the boy–girl inter-action of late childhood is typically strained, often involv-ing indirect or overheard indications of attraction, teasing, and 'fooling around'. These patterns may help to prepare children for later romantic relationships. As Schofield notes, however, 'They do not allow the sort of relaxed, extended social interaction which might let students explore mutual interests and lay the foundation for a friendship.' Still, same-sex friends are often relied on to provide advice and support in the 'courtship' process.[22] These patterns create a legacy that is hard for adolescents and adults to shake. Relatively few adults have close friends of the opposite sex,[23] and even lovers and spouses often find it difficult to relate to one another as friends.[24]

As the cleavage between the groups becomes virtually com-plete, boys' and girls' groups also take on a somewhat different character. While boys tend to view the group as a collective entity, emphasizing loyalty and solidarity, girls are more likely to view the group as a network of intimate two-person friendships. Psychologists Elizabeth Douvan and Joseph Adelson suggest that these differences reflect the different needs of the two sexes as they make the transition from childhood to adulthood.[25] A boy needs a group, they maintain, to support him in his quest for autonomy. 'He wants a band of rebels with whom he can identify and to gain the strength he needs for a stance against adult authority.' Girls, in contrast, do not defy authority as openly and therefore do not value the soli-darity of the group as much as boys. Instead, because of their special concern with emotional intimacy, girls view their groups as a set of close friends, to serve as 'a source of support and a repository of confidences, but not as an ally in open rebellion'.

Although Douvan's and Adelson's distinction may be overdrawn, their analysis is consistent with a variety of

observations of boys' and girls' groups.[26] There is, for
example, a well-documented tendency for boys to congre-
gate in large groups more often than girls, and for girls to
be found in pairs more often than boys. This difference
has been observed in several cultures and in age groups
ranging from five to eleven.[27] And the contrast between
the boys' 'band of rebels' and the girls' 'intimate confi-
dantes' emerges in many descriptions of children's social
relationships.

The prototype of the boys' group as a band of rebels
against adult authority is the delinquent gang – far more
common among boys than among girls – which sometimes
expresses its challenge to the elder generation in violent
form. But the same challenge is expressed, in diluted ways,
by nondelinquent groups of boys as well. For example, the
suburban boys observed by Gary Fine commonly played
such 'harmless' pranks as throwing eggs at houses, ringing
doorbells and then running away, and the 'Polish rope
trick', in which two boys hold an imaginary rope across
a road at nightfall, hoping to stop cars. Recalling his childhood in rural Pennsylvania in the 1910s, the psychologist
B. F. Skinner reports on close variants of these pranks:

> We moved porch furniture from one house to another,
> or hoisted a chair or two into a tree with a length of
> clothesline someone was thoughtless enough to leave
> outdoors. We jammed toothpicks into doorbells so that
> they rang continuously, and ran away before anyone
> could reach the door . . . We also tied tin cans in groups
> of three or four and concealed them on opposite sides
> of the sidewalk with a string running between them high
> enough to catch the ankle of an unsuspecting pedestrian.[28]

It is always 'we' who engage in such exploits, never 'I';
the boys need group support in order to break the rules
of adult society. Such rebellion seems to be less common

and less overt among girls.

For their part, girls' greater concern with intimate, two-person friendships has frequently been noted. In an extensive study of American ten-year-olds in both city and suburban schools, sociologist Janet Lever concluded that girls tended to feel most comfortable when they were with a single best friend. 'There is usually an open show of affection between these little girls,' Lever reports, 'both physically in the form of hand-holding and verbally through "love-notes" that reaffirm how special each is to the other.'[29] And even when girls get together in groups, the tone is more likely to be one of intimacy than of rebellion. A twelve-year-old girl reports, for example: 'Naomi had a party on Saturday (sleep over). We had true confessing and everyone told their secrets. Then we felt so close! We hugged each other and said we loved each other. Some people cried.' Although boys are likely to have best friends as well, their friendships tend to be less intimate and expressive than girls'. Hand-holding and love-notes are virtually unknown among boys, and the confidences that boys share are more likely to be 'group secrets' than expressions of private thoughts and feelings.

Along with their greater concern with intimacy, girls have been found to be more exclusive than boys, in the sense that they are less likely to expand their two-person friendships to include a third person.[30] Girls appear to have a more acute appreciation than boys of the fragility of intimate relationships and of the ways in which one friendship may sometimes threaten another. Eleven-year-old Sarah reports: 'Joan's now trying to hang around the older kids so as to be admitted into their gang so she has no time to be with Liz who therefore tries to be friends with Christine which doesn't please Sally.' Boys, who may be more concerned than girls with the dominance hierarchies of their groups,[31] are typically less sensitive to such dilemmas of intimacy. And because of girls' greater concern with intimacy, jealousy seems more likely to arise in girls' than in boys' groups.

Why do boys' and girls' friendships differ in these ways? Douvan and Adelson try to explain the difference in terms of a psychoanalytically derived view that boys have a greater need to band together and rebel against paternal authority. Other behavioural scientists have speculated – albeit without solid evidence – that there are biologically based predispositions for males to bond in groups and for females to be concerned with intimate, nurturant relationships.[32] But the different patterns of friendship seem to be best understood as outcomes of early learning experiences. Part of this learning may come from the different games and sports that boys and girls play. Janet Lever observes that girls' games (such as playing house or jumping rope) are likely to involve close contact with a single, well-liked person, whereas boys' games (such as baseball or football) are more likely to be played in larger groups and to call for cooperation even with teammates who may not be well-liked personally.[33]

Whether sex-typed games and sports are viewed as causing the differences or as reflections of already existing differences, it is clear that boys and girls grow up with somewhat different models of social relations. In their intimate friendships, girls develop their aptitude for nurturance and emotional expressiveness, social skills that are most relevant to close personal and family relationships. In their larger groups, boys learn to operate within systems of rules and to get along even with people they don't especially like, social skills that are most relevant to modern organizational life. Each sex learns something of importance, but at the same time each sex is deprived of opportunities to learn other important skills. I suspect, for example, that the social learning of childhood is responsible in large measure for the special difficulty that men often have in forming intimate friendships.[34] My own view is that it would be valuable for both boys and girls to have more positively sanctioned exposure to the games, sports, and social patterns that are typically associated with the other sex, as a means of encouraging the fuller development of individual children's potential for rewarding social relationships.

8/Cross-Age Friendships

Joanna reaches up to ring the doorbell, as Elihu stands a step back and watches her.

'Mrs Rubin,' Joanna says when her ring is answered, 'can Elihu come over to my house?' Permission is granted.

'Come on, Elihu,' Joanna says. She runs into the street, with Elihu following a few steps behind. Joanna abruptly stops and turns around. She gently takes Elihu's hand and they continue across the street together.

'Do you want to play Runny Pogo?' Joanna asks.

'Yeah,' Elihu responds, and waits attentively for further instructions.

'Come on, Elihu,' Joanna yells, as she begins to run back and forth across her front lawn. He follows her at top speed. Then the pattern shifts. Instead of Elihu tailing Joanna, they start at opposite ends of the lawn and criss-cross past one another. Screaming at the top of their lungs, they both fall down and laugh uproariously.

Soon afterwards, Joanna and Elihu go around to the back of her house and climb on her climbing frame. Joanna reaches the top rung first and proclaims, 'I'm the queen.' A moment later Elihu reaches the top rung, opposite her, and carefully pronounces, 'I'm the king.'

Joanna and Elihu are close friends who share many

activities together, especially in the late afternoons when Joanna is home from nursery school. Each is highly responsive to the other, although it is Joanna who more often takes the lead in structuring their activity and Elihu who more often imitates her behaviour. They are friends even though they are not, by any conventional reckoning, peers. Joanna is almost precisely twice Elihu's age: he is two and a quarter and she is four and a half.

Neighbourhood friendships that cross age lines are fairly common – just how common is not really known.[1] But they remain at odds with the more typical pattern of friendship in modern Western countries, where it is generally assumed that children should be associating with others about their own age. This assumption seems to be of relatively recent origin, fostered by the institution of an age-segregated educational system in the mid-nineteenth century.[2] Children spend much of their time in school, meet children of the same age in their classes, and continue these friendships outside school as well. More generally, children of the same age are viewed as 'appropriate' friends, both by adults and by children themselves, whereas children who are more than a little older or younger come to be viewed as inappropriate. Indeed, a child's preference for older or younger friends is likely to be seen as a danger signal – a sign of some psychological or social difficulty.

The emphasis on age-segregation in modern Western society has filtered down from elementary school to earlier ages. Most daycare and other pre-school programmes are age-segregated, with two-year-olds, three-year-olds, and four-year-olds in separate groups. Pre-school teachers sometimes argue, like their grade school counterparts, that the intellectual and social goals of their programmes are most likely to be achieved if all of the children are at approximately the same level of maturity. My wife ran into this assumption when she tried to place Elihu in a pre-school programme before his third birthday:

The first school that I visited was reputed to have a
liberal, progressive atmosphere without rigid rules and
restrictions. The admissions officer (who doubled as the
teacher) was initially pleasant and receptive. But as soon
as I gave her Elihu's birthdate, she gasped in horror.
'Then he won't be a two-nine!'

'He won't be a what?'

'He won't be a two-nine by September. He'll only be
two-eight. He wouldn't be able to handle our programme.'

'Oh,' I said, regretting my lack of foresight in not
having given birth 27 days earlier, in order to accelerate
my son's intellectual development.[3]

If the age-segregation of children's social lives has been
inspired by educators, it has undoubtedly been fostered
by parents as well. When they move into new neighbourhoods, parents often make sure not only that there are other
children but that there are other children of the same age,
so that their sons and daughters 'can make friends'. The
emphasis on age-grading is reflected even in the playgroups that parents set up for their infants and toddlers.
In this context, a fourteen-month-old is likely to be considered too old for a group of nine-month-old infants, and
too young for a group of two-year-old toddlers. His only
recourse (or that of his mother) may be to find a group
of 'in-betweens' like himself – again, so he can make
friends.

The concern with getting children together with their
agemates is in tune with a more general cultural pre-
occupation with children's age as an index of their capacities
and privileges. There are books about *Your Two-Year-Old*,
Your Three-Year-Old, and so on, which may create the
impression that with each birthday the child is abruptly
thrust into a new intellectual and social world. And, in
some respects, she is. American children are sent to nursery

school at three, to kindergarten at five, to first grade at six. There are specific ages at which they are allowed to take books out of the library, go to the cinema alone, pay full fare on public transport. (And the progression continues. In Massachusetts, children – now adolescents – are allowed to drive at sixteen, to vote at eighteen, to drink at twenty. Finally, when they are thirty-five, they can run for President.) This age-consciousness does not, of course, escape the attention of the children themselves. For example:

> Ricky and Josh get into a pushing fight with Caleb. Afterwards Ricky explains to me why they don't want to play with him: 'Because we're all big guys and he's little. We're four and we can beat him up.'
> 'Uh, uh,' Caleb objects, 'I'm three and three quarters.'
> 'I was told you're *almost* four,' Ricky coolly answers. 'When you're going to be four, I'm going to be five and you can't beat me up.'

In this instance, the age difference seems to be more of a rationalization for excluding Caleb than the actual reason for it. But even its availability for such rationalization points to the power that age-grading is likely to assume in children's social lives.

By the middle and later years of childhood, such age-consciousness can be especially intense. One thirteen-year-old who transferred to a new school, where she was one of the oldest in her class, sent her teacher an impassioned complaint:

> The kids are really irritating me. Before vacation I had sort of gotten on their level and I could talk to them and have a great time, sort of. Now after a whole vacation of being with my *friends* I can't stand these kids – I feel like I'm in sixth grade again – what a pain – I wish to

God there was someone my age here. I mean – you know – shit I'm so irritated...[4]

Despite the prevalence of this age-segregated state of affairs, the widespread assumption that it is the most 'natural' and, accordingly, most desirable arrangement has been challenged. From an anthropologist's perspective, the age-grading of children's social contacts in modern Western societies is an anomaly. In most of the world's cultures – at least until very recent shifts towards the Western pattern – children have usually played and socialized in mixed-age groups. Among the Nyansongo of Kenya, for example, early childhood groups consist of siblings, cousins, and other relatives from neighbouring homesteads, with widely dispersed ages. In the Okinawan village of Taira, the daily 'kindergarten' group includes all children from weaning age up to the age of six.[5] After surveying the data on infants' and young children's interactions in nonhuman primate species and in non-Western societies, anthropologist Melvin Konner goes so far as to speculate that young children have a genetically built-in predisposition to associate with non-agemates. This predisposition is thwarted by the age-segregated patterns of Western society. 'The apes and prohominids went to considerable trouble to evolve for us a successful childhood in non-peer play groups,' Konner writes. '[This perspective] urges us to wonder a little what may be the cost to our children of keeping them so much of the time with children precisely their own age.'[6] And, regardless of the merits of such an evolutionary argument, many Western researchers and educators have been moving to the view that we too should encourage such mixed-age interaction, as a means of increasing the opportunities and benefits of children's friendships.

It should be stressed that no one is arguing against same-age friendships. To the contrary, as Willard Hartup points out, same-age friendships are always likely to have special importance for children because of their fundamentally egalitarian nature.[7] When two children are of approximately the same age and degree of competence, neither can be assumed to be the leader or authority in their interactions. Instead, they start at an equal level, with distinctions of status emerging only as a result of the children's own negotiations and discoveries about themselves. The potential for intimacy – for becoming real 'chums' – seems likely to be greatest among children who can identify with one another as equals, facing common challenges and concerns. Even young children are apparently aware of this special potential. Within mixed-age daycare centres and nursery schools, children remain likely to establish their closest ties with children of their own age.[8]

In mixed-age settings, friendships with older and younger children do not replace same-age friendships. But relationships that cross age lines can supplement same-age contacts in beneficial ways. For one thing, children who are 'equals' in a particular domain – whether it is physical size or verbal fluency or athletic skills – are not always of the same age. For three-year-old Suzanne, who is large for her age and sometimes frightens off other three-year-olds, association with four-year-olds may prove to be more rewarding. For five-year-old Pedro, a newcomer to the United States who has never before spoken English, interaction with three-year-olds – themselves less fluent in English – may be the best way to gain entry into the group.[9] An important advantage of mixed-age settings, whether they are pre-schools, multi-age elementary school classrooms, clubs, teams, or neighbourhoods, is that they allow children greater flexibility in finding their 'peers'.

Even when children of different ages are not peers, however, they can often establish uniquely rewarding relationships. Same-age groups often breed competition and aggressiveness, as individual children strive to be the strongest or most successful among their peers. Interaction across age lines may help to diffuse this competition. In her pioneering study of social interaction in nursery school, conducted in the 1930s, Lois Barclay Murphy found that hostile acts were most prevalent in a group of three-year-olds with a narrow age range, whereas sympathetic responses were most prevalent in a group which included both 'big children' (three-and-a-half- to four-year-olds) and 'babies' (two-year-olds).[10] Such mixed-age interaction can provide younger children with the stimulation and guidance of their elders, and older children with the sense of pride and responsibility that comes from helping others.

Pre-school educator Helene Rand offers the example of John, who was a bully in his school's four-year-old group. He wanted to dominate his peers, both physically and verbally, and behaved in a very competitive, hostile way. The daycare centre's subsequent switch to mixed-age grouping gave John the opportunity to exercise leadership more gently and appropriately:

> As he watched a two-and-a-half-year-old struggling to put on a jacket, he approached the frustrated toddler, offered help, and said, 'It's okay. When I was little I couldn't do that. I'll help you. I'll take care of you today. I will be your friend.' During the outdoor time, John led the toddler to the sandbox, set up play materials for him and spent the rest of the morning showing his younger friend how to make tunnels in the sand.[11]

Whereas John's competitive encounters with children of his own age were often disapproved of, he was admired by the younger children he helped and praised by adults. The result was to increase John's sense of competence and, ultimately, to facilitate his relationships with children of his own age as well.

Laboratory studies in which same-age and cross-age pairs or groups are created and compared have demonstrated that even young children have a remarkably good capacity to adjust their style of interaction to the cross-age situation. When four-year-old children are given the task of explaining the workings of a toy to a two-year-old, they use short, direct explanations that the toddler can comprehend, quite unlike the more complex descriptions they provide to adults or even to fellow four-year-olds. For example, a four-year-old boy explains to a two-year-old girl:

Lookit, Patty. Hi, Patty. We got an ark. Looka! Isn't that fun? We can put lots of animals on back. Can't you want animals?

(Demonstrating) See? That's the way. Two hands around it.[12]

There is also reason to believe that such interactions with older pre-schoolers can enhance the toddler's own conversational repertoire. In one recent study, toddlers were found to engage in more conversations with other children in family daycare settings where three- and four-year-olds were present than in group daycare settings inhabited only by fellow toddlers.[13]

Not only do young children accommodate themselves successfully to the demands of cross-age interaction, but they also seem to enjoy it. Even before their first birthdays babies are specially fascinated by children older than themselves, and older children in turn enjoy the attention and adulation they receive from younger ones. The following episode involving two brothers is illustrative:

Tim (aged 33 months) jumps and falls. Robert (aged 8 months) watches, roars with laughter. Mutual look,

Tim jumps and falls again, saying, 'Look, Rob, look at me,' continues to jump and fall around room, laughing too, repeated mutual looks and laughter.[14]

As babies become toddlers who can run and jump themselves, their rapt interest in their elders persists, and it is coupled with an increasing amount of direct imitation. At fourteen months, for example, Elihu joins three-year-old Mia, six-year-old Deborah, and seven-year-old Rebecca as they all repeatedly jump up and down, turn in circles, and shout 'Yeah, yeah, yeah!' in time to rock music that is blaring from the television set. Elihu keeps his eyes on the older girls, a big smile on his face, and never loses the beat. In many instances, indeed, babies and toddlers are more interested in monitoring and imitating the behaviour of older children than that of adults. Other children may be viewed as less threatening and more 'like me' than adults, even as they are more interesting and responsive than other babies. And older children are often able and willing to persist in the jumping, hiding, running, and chasing games that the toddler can enjoy for far longer than most adults would be able to manage.

Through such joint activities, the younger child can acquire a wide range of skills from her elders, including skills that seem to be of practical value (such as climbing on a chair to reach the sink) and skills that seem to be of no value at all (such as blowing cake crumbs out of one's mouth). At two and a half, Elihu, having dinner with his mother and father, puts his fingers in the corners of his mouth, pulls them out into a monsterlike grin, and shouts 'Heh, heh, heh, heh!' in an ominous tone. He turns to us and says sweetly, 'Joanna showed me that.' Whether or not the skills imparted have any redeeming value, they testify to the power of older children as socializers of behaviour.

Older pre-schoolers are also likely to show considerable empathy for younger ones. When Elihu is crying, for example, Joanna comforts him resourcefully:

'Want some pizza?' Joanna asks.
'No, I don't want pizza,' Elihu says through his tears.
'Want to ride on my bicycle?' Joanna offers.
'No, I don't want to ride on a bicycle,' Elihu says, tears still streaming down.
'Want to see a dragon?' Joanna asks in a conspiratorial tone, putting her arm around him.
'Yeah,' Elihu replies, his expression shifting almost instantly from a sorrowful frown to an eager smile.

In cross-age nursery schools, similarly, one is likely to observe a variety of attempts by older children to console, entertain, and help to take care of their younger classmates.

Girls seem more likely than boys to play this sort of nurturant role towards younger children. In an Edinburgh nursery school observed by W. C. McGrew, four-year-old girls were more likely than boys to attend to and comfort the three-year-olds who had just entered the group. In response to one boy's evident anxieties, a four-year-old 'little mother' explained in soothing tones, 'All the Mummies come back after milk – when the bell rings.' Girls also made use of physical contact to comfort the younger children – holding their hands, patting their backs, gently hugging their shoulders.[15] Other studies have found older sisters to be more sensitive than older brothers to the needs of their younger siblings, and more patient and effective as teachers.[16] There is no doubt that boys are capable of such nurturant behaviour as well, however. It can be argued, indeed, that the opportunity to interact with younger children is especially important for boys in a society which otherwise does its best to foster boys' competitive strivings and to dampen their nurturant capacities.

As children enter the elementary school years, they

remain capable of fine-tuning their behaviour to meet the requirements of cross-age interaction. In one experiment, three-child groups of varying age composition were given the task of building a tower together. When one eight-year-old was paired with two six-year-olds, the eight-year-old spontaneously took the role of teacher, assuming the major responsibility for directing the activity. In these situations, the six-year-olds' own building performance did not suffer. On the contrary, their block-building skills were probably sharpened by the chance to work with an older child.[17]

These benefits of cross-age interaction are increasingly being exploited in tutoring programmes set up in some American elementary schools – where, for example, fifth-graders (ten-year-olds) volunteer to tutor first- and second-graders (six- and seven-year-olds) on a regular basis. Evaluations of such programmes have shown that they can be of great benefit to both children. The tutee gains both individualized instruction and an older friend who can serve as a model. The tutor gains experience in accommodating himself to another person's level and in taking responsibility for another person's well-being.[18] As one Michigan fifth-grader proudly reported, 'Tutoring is having to cope with kids' problems when they don't understand and it especially makes me feel important because I get to teach someone else.'[19]

Many of the advantages of cross-age interaction that we have discussed may be observed most dramatically in the interactions of brothers and sisters. Throughout the childhood years, older siblings often take a special interest in the well-being of their little brothers and sisters. A four-year-old big brother or sister will proudly pick up the baby, play gently with him, and offer toys or food when he is crying. As the children grow up together, the older child will help the younger with her school work, coach her in athletics, or advise her about social relations. The experience of assisting a younger brother or sister may help the older child to become a more caring and sympathetic person outside the family as well. Studies in several cultures have found that children who have younger siblings tend to be more helpful and nurturant than children who do not.[20] Younger siblings, for their part, not only receive help from their big brothers and sisters but also must learn to get along with these more powerful and sometimes domineering figures. It may be as a result of this learning that later-born children seem to be slightly more socially skilled and better liked than first-borns.[21]

Despite the potential benefits of having a brother or sister, however, parents frequently bemoan the failure of their children to become friends. Although brothers and sisters are sometimes extremely close, in many other cases their relationships seem to be characterized more by hostility than by friendship, and with the passage of time siblings often grow apart from one another.[22] The difficulty that brothers and sisters often have in forming close relationships is usually attributed to sibling rivalry – the intense competition that children feel because of their need to share the love and attention of their parents. But whereas rivalry between siblings is always present, I doubt that it is the main reason for the frequent failure of siblings to become friends. The cultural emphasis on age-segregation is also part of the explanation. One college student recalls what is probably a common state of affairs:

> I was the older sister and, the way I remember it, there was not much reinforcement given to my younger sister when she wanted to be included in my play with my same-age friends. When she was included, it was usually out of obligation to my younger sister. She was put in the role of 'baby' or 'tag-along', and my friends and I must have made her feel fairly unwanted and out of

> place. Because of my role as 'the big one', I felt it was
> an imposition to have to accommodate my younger
> sister to my play relationships. As I look back, I
> remember feeling that it was just more 'natural' for
> children to be playing with other children their own
> age.[23]

In such an age-conscious atmosphere, in which brothers
and sisters are likely to be excluded from each other's
groups of friends, the possibilities for close friendships
between siblings are inevitably diminished.

Cross-age friendships will, of course, have their negative
as well as their positive side. Such alliances may sometimes
lead to the bullying of a younger child by an older one, or
to the rejection of an older child by her own peers because
she has a younger friend. Parents or teachers may sometimes fear that a cross-age friendship is leading a younger
child to engage in activities that he is not yet ready for
or is causing an older child to 'regress' to an immature
style of behaviour. And an older child herself may lose
interest in a younger friend and then drop him abruptly.
There may also be cases in which a child's exclusive
preference for older or younger friends really is a danger
signal that adults should attend to. One example is the
child who seeks out friendships with older children 'because he has to put himself into situations in which he's
sure to lose and have a ready reason for it'.[24] But these
dangers of cross-age friendships are, in my view, out-
weighed by their potential advantages.

We have already seen many of these benefits, to older
and younger children alike. Anthropologist Beatrice Whiting places them in a broader perspective. In societies in
which cross-age interaction is the norm, she notes, children
come to be less dependent and demanding with their
parents, less individualistic and competitive, and more
concerned with the welfare of their community than do

children in Western societies. 'To take a lesson from tribal societies,' Whiting concludes, 'we need to encourage the young to feel responsible for siblings and younger community members, to feel responsible for the welfare of the social group.'[25] Cross-age interaction, she believes, has the effect of extending our children's sense of communal involvement and responsibility. By giving our children the opportunities and encouragement to make friends across age lines, we may not only be expanding their individual social worlds but also increasing the level of concern and fellowship in our society.

9/Environment and Friendship

In one nursery school, children's social lives revolve around tightly knit, exclusive pairs; in another nursery school, a communal spirit prevails. In one neighbourhood, children's activities with their friends tend to be pre-planned and formal; in another neighbourhood, they are unplanned and spontaneous. In one cultural milieu, friendships shift rapidly; in another milieu, they tend to endure. Such contrasts call our attention to the links between the environments that children inhabit and the forms that their friendships take. The physical features, populations, and social expectations of these settings establish – and, at the same time, limit – the child's opportunities to meet potential friends, and they create and enforce specific patterns of interaction that influence the character of these friendships.

Behavioural scientists have not given sufficient attention to the impact of environment on a child's social life. Most investigations of children's social behaviour are confined to a single setting – usually a school classroom or, more often, a psychologist's laboratory. In studies of this sort, environmental influences are likely to be ignored. Recently, however, there has been a heightened interest in examining human development as it unfolds in its real-life settings, including the child's school, neighbourhood, and culture.[1]

Consider, for example, the ways in which two different

nursery school settings affect children's social lives. The University Nursery School and the Little Nursery School are both half-day nursery schools attended by three- to four-year-olds, mainly from middle-class families, and staffed by experienced and dedicated teachers. The University Nursery School, which we have been looking in on through the course of this book, has twenty-five children, four teachers, and spacious facilities. The Little Nursery School, in contrast, has only six children, a single teacher, and a more compact physical layout. In addition to their difference in size, the two schools differ in the degree to which children's activities are regulated. At the University Nursery School, the children are permitted to roam freely from one activity to another, whether by themselves or with others. At any given time, there are individuals, pairs, and groups dispersed throughout the indoor and outdoor areas, engaged in pursuits of their own choosing. Even during a group storytelling and song time at the end of the morning, children often leave the room to engage in other activities. At the Little Nursery School, the children's activities are much more highly structured. The six boys and girls usually stay together in the same area and activity, under the teacher's direct supervision. When it is swimming time, all six change into their bathing suits and troop outside to the wading pool, and when it is song time all six cluster around the piano while the teacher plays and leads the singing. Part of each morning is devoted to free time, when the children can choose their own activities, but even then they all stay in the same room and the teacher participates actively in their endeavours.

The physical and social environments of these two nursery schools are clearly linked to the character of the children's social relations. At the University Nursery School, there are many potential playmates, and the children are left to make their own decisions about what to do and whom to do it with. Issues of inclusion and exclusion, of making friends and keeping them, are among their central concerns. And although some children are more successful than others in their efforts to make friends, through the course of the year virtually all of them become involved in one or more distinctive friendships or cliques, some ephemeral and some enduring. At the Little Nursery School, in contrast, the group is small enough to allow the children to get to know all of their classmates without much effort. Since most activities are engaged in collectively, under the teacher's protective aegis, issues of inclusion and exclusion rarely arise. Rather than forming distinctive friendships or cliques, the children seem to form an allegiance to the group as a whole, coupled with a strong attachment to their teacher. Whereas children at the University Nursery School get into conflicts that arise from excluding others from their activities, children at the Little Nursery School get into conflicts that arise from their competition for the teacher's attention.

In an ambitious attempt to look more systematically at the ways in which pre-school environments structure children's social lives, psychologists Peter Smith and Kevin Connolly established their own half-day nursery schools (or playgroups) for three- and four-year olds in a church hall in Sheffield.[2] Within this context, they were able to vary the group's size and procedures, and then to make detailed observations of how these variations affected the children's patterns of social interaction. In a small class of ten children, Smith and Connolly found, almost all of the children were part of a single close-knit group, and there were few indications of exclusive pairs or cliques. But when the same group of ten children was merged into a larger class, with a total of twenty-nine children, the close-knit group became dispersed and children became more likely to interact in small groups. In addition, close 'buddy' relationships seemed more likely to develop in the large class. It seems that in small classes, all the children can get to know each other and there is little pressure to make exclusive and discriminating friendship choices. In larger groups, pairing and cliquing becomes more necessary, to ensure that children will have regular playmates.[3]

In other experimental efforts, Smith and Connolly varied the degree to which teachers actively structured the children's activities. Under a 'structured-activities regime', the teachers organized and took part in such activities as clay modelling, picture dominoes, and playing house. Under a 'free-play regime', the children chose their own activities and the teachers had a largely caretaking role. After an eight-month experimental period, both groups were switched to an intermediate arrangement, combining opportunities for both free play and teacher-structured activity. The researchers concluded that each of the two programmes had its own unique advantages. The structured-activity regime increased the children's ability to concentrate on activities for a long period of time, an increase that was sustained even in the postexperimental period when there was less adult involvement. On the other hand, the greater experience of interaction with other children provided by the free-play regime seemed to provide the children with better skills for resolving interpersonal conflicts.

In still other variations of their large-scale experiment, the Sheffield investigators examined the impact of the physical space and resources of a nursery school on patterns of social interaction. When they systematically varied the amount of play space available per child, Smith and Connolly found few differences in the children's behaviour when there were twenty-five, fifty, or seventy-five square feet per child, with the exception that there was less running around in the smaller space. When the space was reduced to as little as fifteen square feet per child for a few sessions, however, there was some increase in aggression and a decrease in the overall amount of social inter-action. Connolly and Smith note that their findings provide support for the twenty-five-square-feet per child lower limit which is recommended by many local authorities in England. But whereas varying the amount of play space did not have a major impact on social behaviour, varying the amount of play equipment available had striking effects. On any given morning, the children found that either one, two, or three complete sets of play equipment were available. With more equipment, the children tended to disperse more widely and into smaller subgroups; with less equipment they congregated in larger groups. In addition, there were fewer conflicts between children when more equipment was available.

The Sheffield research points up the difficulty of determining conclusively which school settings are 'better' for children's psychological or social well-being. It is sometimes assumed, for example, that small schools are preferable to larger ones because they are more likely to encourage the involvement of all children in activities and to permit teachers to give children more individual attention.[4] But whereas this conclusion may often be justified, the Sheffield study suggests that it is misleading simply to conclude that 'small is beautiful'. By facilitating a culture where children are more likely to form unique friendships, larger groups such as the University Nursery School may have important advantages. Similar trade-offs are involved in the comparison between teacher-structured regimes that provide a greater degree of benevolent protection from the sometimes threatening world of peers and free-play regimes that require the children to do more fending for themselves. And whereas abundant play equipment may help to reduce conflicts, less equipment may help children learn to play together cooperatively.

*

My own feeling is that children's social lives can be enhanced by experiences in a diversity of settings. In a small, teacher-structured setting like that of the Little Nursery School, children do learn to get along with one another, but the learning takes place in a closely supervised, nurturant atmosphere. Especially for younger pre-schoolers, such a family-like environment may be a good place to ease comfortably into the world of other children. But larger, less highly structured pre-school settings allow children to enter the world of peer interactions and friendships most fully, give them a wider range of playmates to choose from, and impel them to work out their own accommodations to the issues of group life.

In choosing or planning pre-school settings, we should also be mindful of children's other habitats, such as their homes and neighbourhoods. Teachers and parents may sometimes be able to create a pre-school environment that complements the other settings that particular children inhabit. As Smith and Connolly suggest, children who play a lot with other children in their neighbourhoods but rarely interact with adults may profit most from a structured pre-school environment, with its emphasis on conversations with adults and persistence at tasks. On the other hand, children who have a good deal of interaction with their parents but little with peers may profit most from a free-play environment. In practice, of course, pre-school settings are likely to contain blends of the various elements we have been discussing. Many nursery schools and daycare facilities include some balance of teacher-structured and free-play activities, and even the group size of a larger setting can be varied by sometimes breaking the group into subgroups. Such a balance, which is in fact found to some extent at both the University Nursery School and the Little Nursery School, is all to the good. The issue then becomes not which sort of setting is preferable, but, rather, what the relative emphasis should be among different elements within a setting. To be sure, many other features of pre-school settings are also likely to affect children's social lives, including the age range of the children in the group, whether the children see each other outside as well as inside school, the degree of stability or turnover among teachers and children, the degree of parent participation in the pre-school setting, and the experience and personal qualities of the teacher.

Another aspect of the environment of friendship, although it is harder to specify and measure, is the style of social interaction that characterizes and is valued by any given culture or subculture. Anthropologist Nancy Graves provides useful illustrations of the ways in which differing social orientations are transmitted from adults to children among the Polynesian and European ethnic groups who live side by side in contemporary New Zealand.[5] The Polynesian style of interaction is 'inclusive': people like to interact in groups, without a great deal of selectivity or jealousy. The European style is 'exclusive': people place a premium on privacy and independence, and interaction is most likely to take place in closely linked pairs.

These contrasting orientations are transmitted to the pre-school child by both teachers and parents. At a Polynesian-run play centre, all of the activities are geared towards common and cooperative play. The Polynesian supervisor, Graves observes, often begins by involving a child in some fascinating endeavour, such as building a castle. She then invites other children to join in ('You want to build, too, Mary? Come on, now!' 'Come on, John, you want to build, too?'), until a group activity is formed. Similarly, a Polynesian mother at the centre deflects her son's attempts to engage her in exclusive interaction and instead tries to involve other children with him. At this centre, children are fed a snack of milk and apples or biscuits in a group while they engage in collective singing and dancing. At a European-run centre, in contrast, the teacher expects the children to choose their own activities and to ask her for help when they need it. Each child has his snack individually, serving himself milk and apples at a little table whenever he chooses. Children are praised by the supervisors for good individual work ('That's a nice necklace you strung!' or 'Oh, look at your painting!') but cooperative efforts, such as the joint building of a block structure, are often ignored. And a European mother ignores other children playing near her and her daughter, and makes no attempts to involve her in group activity.

These teachers and parents are not necessarily putting into practice a consciously held belief that children should be 'group-oriented' or 'individualistic'. Nevertheless, their ideas about the atmosphere appropriate to a school, as well as their own customary patterns of social behaviour, clearly influence their actions towards the children. Moreover, interviews conducted at an ethnically mixed play centre[6] suggest that the mothers' contrasting kinds of behaviour are linked to their values of what a 'good' child is like. Both Polynesian and European mothers were asked to describe the traits they would most like their three-year-old child to have. The responses of Polynesian mothers reflected a concern for getting along in the community – the child should be well-behaved, nonaggressive, sociable, and sharing. The European mothers tended to make individual or child-centred descriptions – the child should be happy, healthy, intelligent, and enquiring. Thus the values of the parental generation are reflected in the ways in which they shape their children's social relations.

As a result of these differing patterns of socialization, the children themselves are likely to adopt relatively inclusive or exclusive patterns of interaction. In grade school, Graves reports, Polynesian children are more ready than Europeans to include other children in their interactions. When two six-year-old Polynesian girls notice that another

girl (in this instance, a European) has been abandoned
by a playmate, they immediately include her in their own
group. They also try to mend the European girl's wounded
feelings by finding the girl who has left her. Such inclusive
behaviour is less likely to be displayed by European
children. Thus patterns of peer interaction pick up where
socialization by parents and teachers leaves off, reinforcing
the differences between the two groups. By the time they
are in high school, Graves observes, Polynesian girls are
more friendly and cooperative than are European girls,
whereas European girls are more independent and
cliquish.

Through repeated lessons and models at home and at
school, then, interpersonal styles and values are transmitted from one generation to the next. Of course, the
interpersonal styles and values of a particular culture may
not be as clear or as widely held as Graves makes them
out to be in New Zealand. In the United States, for
example, the values attached to friendship often seem
terribly confused and contradictory, involving both an
emphasis on easy congeniality and 'getting along', on the
one hand, and an ideal of enduring trust and intimacy,
on the other.[7] Parents, teachers, older brothers and sisters,
and the mass media may all send their own messages about
friendship; and boys and girls may receive rather different
communications. All of these complexities make the trans-
mission of values and styles of friendship an unpredictable
and uneven process. But it cannot be doubted that the
particular styles of friendship that children develop are
influenced to a large degree by the styles and values of
their culture.

Children's friendships are staged and shaped not only in
school settings but also in the neighbourhoods in which
they live. As part of a larger study of the impact of
residential neighbourhoods on children's lives, Mary Berg
and Elliott Medrich examined the friendship patterns of

twelve-year-old children in two very different neighbourhoods of Oakland, California.[8] In Monterey, an almost
exclusively white, affluent neighbourhood with beautiful
homes nestled in the hills, children often live at a considerable distance from their friends, and parents frequently
chauffeur their children to preplanned social activities.
The children also seem to be unusually selective in their
friendships. Many of them report having only one or two
real friends, and they express a desire to choose friends
with whom they have 'something in common'. This relatively formal, exclusive pattern of friendship contrasts
sharply with children's friendships in Yuba, a low-income,
predominantly black, inner-city neighbourhood. Yuba
children typically report that they have four or five close
friends, and they seem willing to admit a wider range of
peers to the status of friendship. Children often move
around the neighbourhood together in large groups. Their
social life is extensive and spontaneous, with their daily
summertime wanderings taking them in and out of recreation centres, stores, and schoolyards, 'jostling, chiding,
and sparring with each other as they walk down the streets'.

The differences between the friendships of Monterey
and Yuba can be attributed in part to the physical features
of the two neighbourhoods. Monterey homes are widely
dispersed and the sloping, windy streets – without side-
walks – make access between friends' homes difficult. The
neighbourhood park and recreation centre are located at
the bottom of the hill, at a considerable distance from
many of the homes. These physical arrangements impede
casual contacts between children and create the need for
advance arrangements and parental assistance. Yuba, on
the other hand, is a crowded area filled with children,
without such barriers as high fences, trees, or large dis-
tances between dwellings. It is an environment that
facilitates contacts among children – indeed, one that
literally throws them together. The physical character-

istics of the two neighbourhoods are, of course, closely linked to the economic resources of the inhabitants. And economic resources have other influences on children's social lives. When children in Monterey want to go swimming, for example, they may arrange to be driven by their parents for an afternoon at one of the country clubs to which neighbourhood families belong. When children in Yuba want to go swimming, a group of them may sneak into an apartment-house swimming pool in the neighbourhood for a quick dunk while the manager is out.

In addition to these physical and economic differences, there are also cultural differences that influence the children's friendships. In the white, affluent subculture of Monterey, children's social relationships are undoubtedly patterned to some extent after their parents' relatively formal, prescheduled social lives, which revolve around events such as dinner parties, organization meetings, and country-club events. In addition, the children acquire what may be an 'upper-middle-class' view of friendship, emphasizing selectivity and psychological compatibility. In this system of values, friends cannot simply be people who live nearby, but must have common interests and values. One Monterey girl, whose best friend happened to live next door, was asked whether proximity was the reason for their close friendship. 'No,' she insisted, 'I choose to be with others who are active like me.' In Yuba, children's social lives seem to be patterned after the more inclusive and spontaneous social character of the black inner-city subculture. Indeed, Medrich's data from a wide range of Oakland neighbourhoods suggests that black children, in general, have a more inclusive social orientation than white children.[9] Even when the 'child density' of neighbourhoods is statistically controlled, black children still report having significantly more friends than white children do. In this connection it is of interest to note that Ricky, the most 'inclusive' – and the most popular – child in the University Nursery School class that I observed,

is black and from Oakland; almost all of his classmates
are white.

The Oakland study, like the other studies we have
considered, points up the tradeoffs that are likely to exist
when we compare the positive and negative impacts of
different settings on children's friendships. Twelve-year-
olds in Monterey, for all the material advantages they
enjoy, are likely to complain that there are not enough
children around and to lament their inability to conduct
their social lives on their own. 'While they can appreciate
the space and quiet,' Berg and Medrich write, 'they are
painfully isolated from the spontaneous and unplanned life
style characteristic of children in other neighbourhoods.'
On the other hand, the 'selective' children of Monterey
may also form deeper friendships than the more inclusive
children of Yuba, and this may well be a compensating
advantage.

In the last analysis, the determination of which schools,
neighbourhoods, or other habitats provide the most
favourable staging grounds for children's friendships
depends on the social values of the observer. What is most
clear, however, is that features of the environment, including physical arrangements, economic resources, and
cultural values and expectations, exert a massive influence
on children's social lives.

Adults are faced with a dilemma when it comes to their
influence on children's friendships. On the one hand,
parents and teachers may believe that friendships are a
child's special domain and they should try not to interfere.
On the other hand, they also want to help children
establish satisfying and stimulating friendships.

The line between helping and interfering is a fine one.
Adults' efforts to shape children's friendships are sometimes taken too far, with negative consequences. Parents
and teachers may put pressure on children to 'make friends'
in ways that lead to an overemphasis on congeniality and

conformity. Or disapproving adults may prevail on children to end friendships that are in fact of great value to the child. In many instances, moreover, our best-intentioned attempts to help children with their friendships seem to go awry. An enthusiastic mother may keep urging her toddler to play with another child in a playgroup, but researchers suspect that such constant encouragement is more distracting than helpful. A concerned teacher may rush in to help pre-schoolers settle a dispute, whereas if she waited a little longer the children might work out a better solution on their own.

With this said, however, it remains clear to me that parents and teachers have important roles to play with regard to children's friendships. I have alluded to aspects of these roles through the course of this book. They include providing opportunities for toddlers and pre-schoolers to interact with their peers, helping children to develop social skills, and providing understanding and support when friendships falter or end. Especially with younger children, adults can make an effort to encourage cross-sex and cross-age interaction. Finally, there may be times when adults must step in and remove a child from a friendship or clique that is doing him harm.

Although parents and teachers should take care not to abuse their influence over children's friendships, they should not disclaim it. We are the ones who choose and organize the settings, including neighbourhoods and schools, in which children meet one another. And our own values about friendships – whether they should be formal or informal, inclusive or exclusive, deep or superficial – are unmistakably conveyed to our children, through the examples we set in our relationships with others. Thus we cannot help influencing our children. We can only try to exert this influence wisely and thoughtfully, with a clear view of the special place of friendships in each child's life.

References

1 DO FRIENDS MATTER?

1. Susan Isaacs, *Social Development in Young Children* (New York: Harcourt, Brace, 1939), p. 11.
2. See, for example, Leon Festinger, 'A Theory of Social Comparison Processes', *Human Relations*, 1954, 7, 117–40.
3. For example, Frieda Fromm-Reichmann, 'Loneliness', *Psychiatry*, 1959, 22, 1–15.
4. Katherine H. Read, *The Nursery School*, 6th ed. (Philadelphia: Saunders, 1976), p. 340.
5. See, for example, William A. Corsaro, 'Friendship in the Nursery School: Social Organization in a Peer Environment', in Steven R. Asher and John M. Gottman, eds., *The Development of Children's Friendships* (Cambridge University Press, in press).
6. Robert S. Weiss, 'The Provisions of Social Relationships', in Zick Rubin, ed., *Doing Unto Others: Joining, Molding, Conforming, Helping, Loving* (Englewood Cliffs, N.J.: Prentice-Hall, 1974).
7. See Robert S. Weiss, *Loneliness: The Experience of Emotional and Social Isolation* (Cambridge: MIT Press, 1973). See also Zick Rubin, 'Seeking the Cure for Loneliness', *Psychology Today*, October 1979.
8. Harry Stack Sullivan, *The Interpersonal Theory of Psychiatry* (New York: Norton, 1953), p. 228.

9. Sullivan, *The Interpersonal Theory of Psychiatry*, p. 228.
10. Emory L. Cowen, Andreas Pederson, Haroutun Babigian, Louis D. Izzo, and Mary Anne Trost, 'Long-term Follow-up of Early Detected Vulnerable Children', *Journal of Consulting and Clinical Psychology*, 1973, *41*, 438–46.
11. Henry S. Maas, 'Preadolescent Peer Relations and Adult Intimacy', *Psychiatry*, 1968, *31*, 161–72.
12. William Damon, *The Social World of the Child* (San Francisco: Jossey-Bass, 1977), p. 160.

2   THE EARLIEST FRIENDSHIPS

1. For overviews of research on infants' and toddlers' peer relations, see Edward Mueller and Deborah Vandell, 'Infant–Infant Interaction', in Joy D. Osofsky, ed., *Handbook of Infant Development* (New York: Wiley–Interscience, 1979), and various chapters in Michael Lewis and Leonard A. Rosenblum, eds., *Friendship and Peer Relations* (New York: Wiley–Interscience, 1975). I have also profited from the review provided by Joseph L. Jacobson in 'The Determinants of Early Peer Interaction' (diss., Harvard University, 1977).
2. Edward Mueller and Adrienne Rich, 'Clustering and Socially-Directed Behaviors in a Playgroup of 1-Year-Old Boys', *Journal of Child Psychology and Psychiatry*, 1976, *17*, 315–22.
3. Edward Mueller and Thomas Lucas, 'A Developmental Analysis of Peer Interaction Among Toddlers', in Lewis and Rosenblum, *Friendship and Peer Relations*.
4. Carol O. Eckerman and Judith L. Whatley, 'Toys and Social Interaction Between Infant Peers', *Child Development*, 1977, *48*, 1645–56.
5. Marian Radke Yarrow, 'Some Perspectives on Research on Peer Relations', in Lewis and Rosenblum,

Friendship and Peer Relations, p. 302. For evidence of toddlers' social sensitivity, also see Carolyn Zahn-Waxler, Marian Radke Yarrow, and Robert A. King, 'Child Rearing and Children's Prosocial Initiations Toward Victims of Distress', *Child Development*, 1979, 50, 319–30.

6. Mueller and Lucas, 'A Developmental Analysis of Peer Interaction Among Toddlers', p. 241.

7. See, for example, Wanda C. Bronson, 'Developments in Behavior with Age-Mates During the Second Year of Life', in Lewis and Rosenblum, *Friendship and Peer Relations*.

8. Mueller and Lucas, 'A Developmental Analysis of Peer Interaction Among Toddlers', p. 241.

9. Edward Mueller and Jeffrey Brenner, 'The Origins of Social Skills and Interaction Among Playgroup Toddlers', *Child Development*, 1977, 48, 854–61.

10. Michael Lewis, Gerald Young, Jeanne Brooks, and Linda Michalson, 'The Beginning of Friendship', in Lewis and Rosenblum, *Friendship and Peer Relations*.

11. Bronson, 'Developments in Behavior with Age-Mates During the Second Year of Life', p. 149

12. For a description of young children's conversations, see Catherine Garvey, *Play* (Cambridge: Harvard University Press), pp. 59–76.

13. Judith Rubenstein and Carollee Howes, 'The Effects of Peers on Toddler Interaction with Mother and Toys', *Child Development*, 1976, 47, 597–605.

14. See Zick Rubin, *Liking and Loving: An Invitation to Social Psychology* (New York: Holt, Rinehart and Winston, 1973), chap. 6, ('Familiarity Breeds Content: The Effects of "Mere Exposure"').

15. Jerome Kagan, Richard B. Kearsley, and Philip R. Zelazo, 'The Emergence of Initial Apprehension to Unfamiliar Peers', in Lewis and Rosenblum, *Friendship*

and Peer Relations. Also Jacobson, 'The Determinants of Early Peer Interaction'.

16. Katharine M. Banham Bridges, 'A Study of Social Development in Early Infancy', *Child Development*, 1933, *4*, 36–49.

17. For example, see Carollee Howes and Edward Mueller, 'Early Peer Friendships: Their Significance for Development', in W. Spiel, ed., *The Psychology of the Twentieth Century* (Zurich: Kindler, in press).

18. Mueller and Vandell, 'Infant–Infant Interaction'.

19. Jacobson, 'The Determinants of Early Peer Interaction'. Lewis, Young, Brooks, and Michalson, 'The Beginning of Friendship'. Deborah Loew Vandell, 'Boy Toddlers' Social Interaction with Mothers, Fathers, and Peers' (diss., Boston University, 1977).

20. Alicia F. Lieberman, 'Preschoolers' Competence with a Peer: Relations with Attachment and Peer Experience', *Child Development*, 1977, *48*, 1277–87. See also Everett Waters, Judith Wippman, and L. Alan Sroufe, 'Attachment, Positive Affect, and Competence in the Peer Group: Two Studies in Construct Validation', *Child Development*, 1979, *50*, 821–9.

21. Deborah Lowe Vandell, 'Effects of a Playgroup Experience on Mother–Son and Father–Son Interaction', *Developmental Psychology*, 1979, *15*, 379–85.

22. For example, Mary M. Shirley, *The First Two Years: A Study of Twenty-Five Babies* (Minneapolis: University of Minnesota Press, 1933). Deborah Lowe Vandell and Edward Mueller, 'Peer Play and Friendships During the First Two Years', In Hugh C. Foot, Anthony J. Chapman, and Jean R. Smith, eds., *Friendship and Childhood Relation* (Wiley, in press). Carollee Howes and Judith L. Rubenstein, 'Influences on Toddler Peer Behavior in Two Types of Daycare' (paper, Harvard University, School of Medicine, 1979).

3   WHAT IS A FRIEND?

1. From William Damon, *The Social World of the Child* (San Francisco: Jossey-Bass, 1977), pp. 160, 164. Elizabeth Douvan and Joseph Adelson, *The Adolescent Experience* (New York: Wiley, 1966), p. 176.
2. Robert Selman, 'Toward a Structural Analysis of Developing Interpersonal Relations Concepts: Research with Normal and Disturbed Preadolescent Boys', in Anne D. Pick, ed., *Minnesota Symposium on Child Psychology*, vol. 10 (Minneapolis: University of Minnesota Press, 1976). Robert Selman and Dan Jaquette, 'Stability and Oscillation in Interpersonal Awareness: A Clinical–Developmental Analysis', in Charles B. Keasey, ed., *Nebraska Symposium on Motivation, 1977* (Lincoln: University of Nebraska Press, 1978).
3. Robert Selman and Dan Jaquette, 'The Development of Interpersonal Awareness' (working draft of manual, Harvard-Judge Baker Social Reasoning Project, 1977).
4. Damon, *The Social World of the Child*, p. 163.
5. Selman and Jaquette, 'The Development of Interpersonal Awareness', p. 132.
6. Selman and Jaquette, 'The Development of Interpersonal Awareness', p. 118.
7. Damon, *The Social World of the Child*, p. 164.
8. Selman and Jaquette, 'The Development of Interpersonal Awareness', p. 144.
9. See, for example, Zick Rubin, *Liking and Loving: An Invitation to Social Psychology* (New York: Holt, Rinehart and Winston, 1973), chap. 10 ('The Nature of Love').
10. Harry Stack Sullivan, *The Interpersonal Theory of Psychiatry* (New York: Norton, 1953), p. 245.
11. See John H. Flavell, 'The Development of Knowledge About Visual Perception', in Keasey, ed., *Nebraska Symposium on Motivation, 1977*.

12. W. J. Livesley and D. B. Bromley, *Person Perception in Childhood and Adolescence* (London: Wiley, 1973).

13. Helaine H. Scarlett, Allan N. Press, and Walter H. Crockett, 'Children's Descriptions of Peers: A Wernerian Developmental Analysis', *Child Development*, 1971, *42*, 439–53.

14. Barbara Hollands Peevers and Paul Secord, 'Developmental Change in Attribution of Descriptive Concepts to Persons', *Journal of Personality and Social Psychology*, 1973, *27*, 120–8.

15. Erving Goffman, *Encounters* (Indianapolis: Bobbs-Merrill, 1961).

16. Selman and Jaquette, 'The Development of Interpersonal Awareness', p. 165.

17. See Thomas J. Berndt, 'Relations Between Social Cognition, Nonsocial Cognition, and Social Behavior: The Case of Friendship', in Lee Ross and John H. Flavell, eds., *New Directions in the Study of Social-Cognitive Development*, in press.

18. For description of friendships in non-Western cultures, see, for example, Robert Brain, *Friends and Lovers* (New York: Basic Books, 1976). Yehudi A. Cohen, 'Patterns of Friendship', in Cohen, ed., *Social Structure and Personality* (New York: Holt, Rinehart and Winston, 1961).

19. For an impressive beginning along these lines, see William A. Corsaro, 'Friendship in the Nursery School: Social Organization in a Peer Environment', in Steven R. Asher and John M. Gottman, eds., *The Development of Children's Friendships* (Cambridge University Press, in press).

20. Katherine H. Read, *The Nursery School*, 6th ed. (Philadelphia: Saunders, 1976), p. 347.

21. Jean Piaget, *The Moral Judgment of the Child* (Glencoe, Ill.: Free Press, 1948), p. 56; originally published in 1932.

22. Lawrence Weiss and Marjorie Fiske Lowenthal, 'Life Course Perspectives on Friendship', in Lowenthal, Majda Turner, David Chiriboga et al., *Four Stages of Life* (San Francisco: Jossey-Bass, 1975).

23. For a discussion of the development of adult social relationships that parallels the stages we have been discussing, see George Levinger and J. Diedrick Snoek, *Attraction in Relationship: A New Look at Interpersonal Attraction* (Morristown, N.J.: General Learning Press, 1972).

4 THE SKILLS OF FRIENDSHIP

1. W. C. McGrew, *An Ethological Study of Children's Behavior* (New York: Academic Press, 1972). See also Martha Putallaz and John Gottman, 'Social Skills and Group Acceptance', in Steven R. Asher and John M. Gottman, eds., *The Development of Children's Friendships* (Cambridge University Press, in press).

2. William A. Corsaro, '"We're Friends, Right?": Children's Use of Access Rituals in a Nursery School', *Language in Society*, 1979, *8*, 315–36.

3. John Gottman, Jonni Gonso, and Brian Rasmussen, 'Social Interaction, Social Competence, and Friendship in Children', *Child Development*, 1975, *46*, 709–18.

4. Carol S. Dweck and Therese E. Goetz, 'Attributions and Learned Helplessness', in John H. Harvey, William Ickes, and Robert F. Kidd, eds., *New Directions in Attribution Research*, vol. 2 (Hillsdale, N.J.: Lawrence Erlbaum Associates, 1979).

5. Lee C. Lee, 'Social Encounters of Infants: The Beginnings of Popularity', paper presented to the International Society for the Study of Behavioral Development (Ann Arbor, Michigan, August 1973).

6. Willard W. Hartup, Jane A. Glazer, and Rosalind

Charlesworth, 'Peer Reinforcement and Sociometric Status', *Child Development*, 1967, *38*, 1017–24.

7. Shirley Moore, 'Correlates of Peer Acceptance in Nursery School Children', *Young Children*, 1967, *22*, 281–97.

8. S. Holly Stocking and Diana Arezzo, *Helping Friendless Children: A Guide for Teachers and Parents* (Boys Town, Nebraska: The Boys Town Center for the Study of Youth Development, 1979).

9. Evelyn Beyer, 'Observing Children in Nursery School Situations', in Lois Barclay Murphy, *Personality in Young Children* (New York: Basic Books, 1956), I, 347.

10. See Wyndol Furman, Donald F. Rahe, and Willard W. Hartup, 'Rehabilitation of Socially-Withdrawn Preschool Children Through Mixed-Age and Same-Age Socialization', *Child Development*, 1979.

11. For a review of such programmes, see Melinda L. Combs and Diana Arezzo Slaby, 'Social-Skills Training with Children', in B. B. Lahey and Alan E. Kazdin, eds., *Advances in Clinical Child Psychology*, vol. 1 (New York: Plenum, 1977). See also Sherri Oden and Steven R. Asher, 'Coaching Children in Social Skills for Friendship Making', *Child Development*, 1977, *48*, 495–506.

12. Stocking and Arezzo, *Helping Friendless Children*.

13. Combs and Slaby, 'Social-Skills Training with Children', p. 165.

14. See Philip G. Zimbardo, *Shyness* (Reading, Mass.: Addison-Wesley, 1977), especially chap. 4 ('Parents, Teachers, and Shy Children').

15. See, for example, Karen K. Dion and Ellen Berscheid, 'Physical Attractiveness and Peer Perception Among Children', *Sociometry*, 1974, *37*, 1–12. L. W. McCraw and J. W. Tolbert, 'Sociometric Status and Athletic Ability of Junior High School Boys', *The Research Quarterly*, 1953, *24*, 72–80. Steven R. Asher, Sherri L. Oden, and John M. Gottman, 'Children's Friendships

in School Settings', in L. G. Katz, ed., *Current Topics in Early Childhood Education*, vol. 1 (Norwood, N.J.: Ablex, 1977).

16. See E. Mavis Hetherington, Martha Cox, and Roger Cox, 'Play and Social Interaction in Children Following Divorce', paper presented to the Society for Research on Child Development (San Francisco, March 1979).

5 BEING FRIENDS

1. For a related discussion, see Robert S. Weiss, 'The Provisions of Social Relationships', in Zick Rubin, ed., *Doing Unto Others: Joining, Molding, Conforming, Helping, Loving* (Englewood Cliffs, N.J.: Prentice-Hall, 1974).

2. For a review of such studies, see Willard W. Hartup, 'Peer Interaction and Social Organization', in Paul H. Mussen, ed., *Carmichael's Manual of Child Psychology*, vol. 2 (New York: Wiley, 1970). Related studies of adults' friendships are summarized in Zick Rubin, *Liking and Loving: An Invitation to Social Psychology* (New York: Holt, Rinehart and Winston, 1973), chap. 7 ('Birds of a Feather: The Attraction of Like to Like').

3. This student's log and those on pp. 74 and 75 were provided by Margaret Stubbs.

4. See Harry Stack Sullivan, *The Interpersonal Theory of Psychiatry* (New York: Norton, 1953). See also John M. Gottman and Jennifer T. Parkhurst, 'A Developmental Theory of Friendship and Acquaintanceship Processes', in W. Andrew Collins, ed., *Minnesota Symposium on Child Psychology*, vol. 13 (Lawrence Erlbaum Associates, in press).

5. Robert W. White, *The Enterprise of Living: Growth and Organization in Personality* (New York: Holt, Rinehart and Winston, 1972), p. 304.

6. Gary Alan Fine, 'The Natural History of Preadolescent Male Friendship Groups', in Hugh C. Foot, Anthony J. Chapman, and Jean R. Smith, eds., *Friendship and Childhood Relations* (Wiley, in press).

⁊. For a discussion of such labelling of friendship among adults, see David Jacobson, 'Fair-Weather Friend: Label and Context in Middle-Class Friendships', *Journal of Anthropological Research*, 1975, *31*, 225–34.

8. For a discussion of the role of such self-disclosure in adult friendships, see Rubin, *Liking and Loving*, chap. 8 ('Becoming Intimate: The Long Road to Commitment').

9. Charlotte Zolotow, *My Friend John* (New York: Harper & Row, 1968).

10. Carl Hindy, 'Children's Friendship Concepts and the Perceived Cohesiveness of Same-Sex Friendship Dyads', senior honours thesis, Brandeis University, 1979.

11. See, for example, Elise Hart Green, 'Friendships and Quarrels Among Preschool Children', *Child Development*, 1933, *3*, 237–52.

12. Robert L. Selman, 'The Child as a Friendship Philosopher', in Steven R. Asher and John M. Gottman, eds., *The Development of Children's Friendships* (Cambridge University Press, in press).

6 LOSING FRIENDS

1. Charlotte Zolotow, *Janey* (New York: Harper & Row, 1973), pp. 5, 7, 16, 23.

2. Personal communication from Margaret Stubbs, February 1979.

3. Harry Stack Sullivan, *The Interpersonal Theory of Psychiatry* (New York: Norton, 1953), pp. 241–2.

4. Louise Bates Ames, quoted by Vance Packard in *A*

Nation of Strangers (New York: David McKay, 1972), p. 237.

5. This student's log and those below and on pp. 86 and 87 were provided by Margaret Stubbs.

6. Packard, *A Nation of Strangers*, p. 239.

7. This reaction was pointed out to me by Malcolm Watson.

8. Robert Selman and Dan Jaquette, 'The Development of Interpersonal Awareness' (working draft of manual, Harvard-Judge Baker Social Reasoning Project, 1977), p. 172.

9. Adapted from Mary Cover Jones, 'Studying the Characteristics of Friends', paper presented at the convention of the American Psychological Association, 1948.

10. Benjamin Spock, 'How Children Make Friends', *Redbook*, March 1975, p. 31.

11. Myron Brenton, 'When Best Friends Part', *Parents Magazine*, May 1978, p. 45.

12. See Zick Rubin, Letitia Anne Peplau, and Charles T. Hill, 'Loving and Leaving: Sex Differences in Romantic Attachments', *Sex Roles*, in press.

13. Iona and Peter Opie, *The Lore and Language of Schoolchildren* (Oxford: Oxford University Press, 1959), p. 324.

14. Brenton, 'When Best Friends Part', pp. 67, 71.

15. For a valuable listing of such books, see Joanne E. Bernstein, *Books to Help Children Cope with Separation and Loss* (New York and London: R. B. Bowker Company, 1977).

7   BOYS, GIRLS, AND GROUPS

1. See Georg Simmel's discussion of the dyad and the larger group, in Kurt H. Wolff, ed., *The Sociology of*

Georg Simmel (New York: Free Press, 1950), p. 123.

2. Helen Faigin, 'Social Behavior of Young Children in the *Kibbutz*', *Journal of Abnormal and Social Psychology*, 1958, 56, 117–29.

3. Patricia P. Minuchin, *The Middle Years of Childhood* (Monterey, California: Brooks/Cole, 1977), pp. 72–3.

4. Robert Selman and Dan Jaquette, 'The Development of Interpersonal Awareness' (working draft of manual, Harvard-Judge Baker Social Reasoning Project, 1977).

5. Gary Alan Fine, 'The Natural History of Preadolescent Male Friendship Groups', in Hugh C. Foot, Anthony J. Chapman, and Jean R. Smith, eds., *Friendship and Childhood Relations* (Wiley, in press).

6. See, for example, Maureen T. Hallinan, 'Patterns of Cliquing Among Youth', in Foot, Chapman, and Smith, *Friendship and Childhood Relations*.

7. Janet Ward Schofield, 'Complementary and Conflicting Identities: Images and Interaction in an Inter-racial School', in Steven R. Asher and John M. Gottman, eds., *The Development of Children's Friendships* (Cambridge University Press, in press).

8. For a review of research on children's conformity to their peers, see Willard W. Hartup, 'Peer Interaction and Social Organization', in Paul H. Mussen, ed., *Carmichael's Manual of Child Psychology*, vol. 2 (New York: Wiley, 1970).

9. Muzafer Sherif and Carolyn Sherif, *Groups in Harmony and Tension* (New York: Harper & Brothers, 1953).

10. Carolyn Wood Sherif, *Orientation in Social Psychology* (New York: Harper & Row, 1976), p. 69.

11. This student's log and those on p. 105 were provided by Margaret Stubbs.

12. Urie Bronfenbrenner, *The Ecology of Human Development* (Cambridge: Harvard University Press, 1979), p. 284.

13. John Condry and Michael L. Siman, 'Characteristics of Peer- and Adult-Oriented Children', *Journal of Marriage and the Family*, 1974, *36*, 543–54.

14. Minuchin, *The Middle Years of Childhood*, p. 73.

15. For example, Donald R. Omark, Monica Omark, and Murray S. Edelman, 'Formation of Dominance Hierarchies in Young Children: Action and Perception', in Thomas R. Williams, ed., *Psychological Anthropology* (The Hague: Mouton, 1975).

16. Carol Nagy Jacklin and Eleanor E. Maccoby, 'Social Behavior at Thirty-three Months in Same-Sex and Mixed-Sex Dyads', *Child Development*, 1978, *49*, 557–569.

17. Recent work with young monkeys lends support to this possibility. See, for example, Leonard A. Rosenblum, Christopher L. Coe, and Lyn J. Bromley, 'Peer Relations in Monkeys: The Influence of Social Structure, Gender, and Familiarity', in Michael Lewis and Leonard A. Rosenblum, eds., *Friendship and Peer Relations* (New York: Wiley–Interscience, 1975).

18. Barbara D. Bianchi and Roger Bakeman, 'Sex-Typed Affiliation Preferences Observed in Preschoolers: Traditional and Open School Differences', *Child Development*, 1978, *49*, 910–12.

19. Lisa A. Serbin, Ilene J. Tonick, and Sarah H. Sternglanz, 'Shaping Cooperative Cross-Sex Play', *Child Development*, 1977, *48*, 924–9.

20. Maureen Hallinan, 'Structural Effects on Children's Friendships and Cliques', *Social Psychology Quarterly*, 1979, *42*, 43–54.

21. Schofield, 'Complementary and Conflicting Identities'. See also Janet Ward Schofield and H. Andrew Sagar, 'Peer Interaction Patterns in an Integrated Middle School', *Sociometry*, 1977, *40*, 130–8.

22. See also Gary Alan Fine, 'Impression Management and Preadolescent Behavior: Friends as Socializers',

in Asher and Gottman, *The Development of Children's Friendships*.

23. For example, Alan Booth and Elaine Hess, 'Cross-Sex Friendship', *Journal of Marriage and the Family*, 1974, *36*, 38–47.

24. See, for example, Henry Grunebaum, 'Thoughts on Sex, Love, and Commitment', *Journal of Sex & Marital Therapy*, 1976, *2*, 277–83.

25. Elizabeth Douvan and Joseph Adelson, *The Adolescent Experience* (New York: Wiley, 1966), pp. 201–2.

26. For a useful review, I am indebted to Nancy Pistrang and Karen Sabovich, 'Sex Differences in Children's Friendships' (unpublished paper, University of California, Los Angeles, 1978).

27. For example, Omark, Omark, and Edelman, 'Formation of Dominance Hierarchies in Young Children'.

28. B. F. Skinner, *Particulars of My Life* (New York: Knopf, 1976), pp. 83–4.

29. Janet Lever, 'Sex Differences in the Games Children Play', *Social Problems*, 1976, *23*, 478–87.

30. For example, Donna Eder and Maureen T. Hallinan, 'Sex Differences in Children's Friendships', *American Sociological Review*, 1978, *43*, 237–50. Norma Feshbach and Gittelle Sones, 'Sex Differences in Adolescent Reactions Toward Newcomers', *Developmental Psychology*, 1971, *4*, 381–6.

31. See Omark, Omark, and Edelman, 'Formation of Dominance Hierarchies in Young Children'. See also Richard C. Savin-Williams, 'An Ethological Study of Dominance Formation and Maintenance in a Group of Human Adolescents', *Child Development*, 1976, *47*, 972–9.

32. For an evolutionary analysis of male bonding, see Lionel Tiger, *Men in Groups* (New York: Random House, 1970).

33. See also John D. Burchard, 'Competitive Youth

Sports and Social Competence', in Martha Whalen Kent and Jon E. Rolf, eds., *Primary Prevention of Psychopathology, Vol. III: Social Competence in Children* (Hanover, New Hampshire: University Press of New England, 1979).

34. See, for example, Alan Booth, 'Sex and Social Participation', *American Sociological Review*, 1972, 37, 183–92. See also Joseph H. Pleck and Jack Sawyer, eds., *Men and Masculinity* (Englewood Cliffs, N.J.: Prentice-Hall, 1974) and Mayta A. Caldwell and Letitia Anne Peplav, 'Sex Differences in Same-Sex Friendship', *Sex Roles*, in press.

8   CROSS-AGE FRIENDSHIPS

1. See, for example, Shari Ellis, Cindy C. Cromer, and Barbara Rogoff, 'Age-Segregation of Children', paper presented to the Society for Research on Child Development (San Francisco, March 1979).

2. Joseph Kett, 'The History of Age Grading in America', in James S. Coleman et al., eds., *Youth: Transition to Adulthood* (Chicago: University of Chicago Press, 1974).

3. Carol Rubin, 'Off to a Good Start', *Boston Globe*, 4 April 1979.

4. From a student's log provided by Margaret Stubbs.

5. Beatrice B. Whiting, ed., *Six Cultures* (New York: John Wiley, 1963).

6. Melvin Konner, 'Relations Among Infants and Juveniles in Comparative Perspective', in Michael Lewis and Leonard A. Rosenblum, eds., *Friendship and Peer Relations* (New York: Wiley–Interscience, 1975), p. 123.

7. Willard W. Hartup, 'Cross-Age Versus Same-Age Peer Interaction: Ethological and Cross-Cultural Perspectives', in Vernon L. Allen, ed., *Children as Teachers:*

Theory and Research on Tutoring (New York: Academic Press, 1976).

8. For example, Carollee Howes and Judith Rubenstein, 'Experience with Pre-Schoolers and Toddler Peer Interaction in Two Types of Daycare', paper presented at the International Conference on Infant Studies (Providence, Rhode Island, March 1978). See also Mildred B. Parten, 'Social Play Among Preschool Children', *Journal of Abnormal and Social Psychology*, 1933, *28*, 136–47.

9. Helene Y. Rand, 'Multi-Age Groups: Let Them Reason Together', *Day Care and Early Education*, March–April 1976, 24–7.

10. Lois Barclay Murphy, *Social Behavior and Child Personality: An Exploratory Study of Some Roots of Sympathy* (New York: Columbia University Press, 1937), pp. 67, 158.

11. Rand, 'Multi-Age Groups', p. 25.

12. Marilyn Shatz and Rochel Gelman, 'The Development of Communication Skills: Modifications in the Speech of Young Children as a Function of Listener', *Monographs of the Society for Research in Child Development*, 1973, *38*, 5, pp. 1–37.

13. Howes and Rubenstein, 'Experience with Pre-Schoolers and Toddler Peer Interaction in Two Types of Daycare'.

14. Judy Dunn and Carol Kendrick, 'Interaction Between Young Siblings in the Context of Family Relationships', in Michael Lewis and Leonard A. Rosenblum, eds., *The Child and Its Family* (New York: Plenum Press, 1979), p. 158.

15. W. C. McGrew, 'Aspects of Social Development in Nursery School Children with Emphasis on Introduction to the Group', in N. Blurton-Jones, ed., *Ethological Studies of Child Behaviour* (London: Cambridge University Press, 1972), p. 139. Also see the examples

provided by Murphy in *Social Behavior and Child Personality*.

16. Victor C. Cicirelli, 'Siblings Teaching Siblings', in Allen, *Children as Teachers*. Rona Abramovitch, Carl Corter, and Bella Lando, 'Sibling Interaction in the Home', paper presented to the Society for Research on Child Development (San Francisco, March 1979).

17. William Graziano, Doran French, Celia A. Brownell, and Willard W. Hartup, 'Peer Interaction in Same- and Mixed-Age Triads in Relation to Chronological Age and Incentive Condition', *Child Development*, 1976, 47, 707–14.

18. Vernon L. Allen, 'The Helping Relationship and Socialization of Children: Some Perspectives on Tutoring', in Allen, *Children as Teachers*.

19. Roberta Fairleigh, 'Cross-Age Caring', *Teacher*, December 1978.

20. Ervin Staub, *The Development of Prosocial Behavior in Children* (Morristown, N.J.: General Learning Press, 1975). Beatrice B. Whiting and John W. M. Whiting, *Children of Six Cultures* (Cambridge: Harvard University Press, 1975), p. 134.

21. Norman Miller and Geoffrey Maruyama, 'Ordinal Position and Peer Popularity', *Journal of Personality and Social Psychology*, 1976, 33, 123–31.

22. There has been very little research on children's relationships with their siblings. For a recent overview, see Jay D. Schvaneveldt and Marilyn Ihinger, 'Sibling Relationships in the Family', in Wesley R. Burr, Reuben Hill, F. Ivan Nye, and Ira L. Reiss, eds., *Contemporary Theories About the Family*, vol. 1 (New York: Free Press, 1979).

23. Beth Lipstein, log for Psychology 138, Brandeis University, Spring 1979.

24. Geraldine Youcha, 'Making Friends', *Parents Magazine*, February 1976, p. 46.

25. Beatrice B. Whiting, 'The Dependency Hangup and Experiments in Alternative Life Styles', in J. Milton Yinger and Stephen J. Cutler, eds., *Major Social Issues: A Multidisciplinary View* (New York: Free Press, 1978), p. 226. A similar argument is made by Urie Bronfenbrenner in *Two Worlds of Childhood: U.S. and U.S.S.R.* (New York: Touchstone Books, 1972).

9   ENVIRONMENT AND FRIENDSHIP

1. See Urie Bronfenbrenner, *The Ecology of Human Development* (Cambridge: Harvard University Press, 1979).

2. Kevin Connolly and Peter Smith, 'Experimental Studies of the Preschool Environment', *International Journal of Early Childhood*, 1978, *10*, 86–95. A full account of this research is presented in Peter K. Smith and Kevin J. Connolly, *The Ecology of Preschool Behaviour* (Cambridge University Press, in press).

3. See William A. Corsaro, 'Friendship in the Nursery School: Social Organization in a Peer Environment', in Steven R. Asher and John M. Gottman, eds., *The Development of Children's Friendships* (Cambridge University Press, in press).

4. See, for example, Bronfenbrenner, *The Ecology of Human Development*, pp. 191–5, 202. See also Paul V. Gump, 'School Environments,' in Irwin Altman and Joachim F. Wohlwill, eds., *Children and the Environment* (New York: Plenum Press, 1978).

5. Nancy B. Graves, 'Inclusive Versus Exclusive Interaction Styles in Polynesian and European Classrooms: In Search of an Alternative to the Cultural Deficit Model of Learning'. Research Report No. 5, March 1974.

6. Edite Denée, 'Mother–Child Interaction at an Ethni-

cally Mixed Auckland Play Centre – An Exploratory Study' (master's thesis, University of Auckland, 1973). Cited by Graves in 'Inclusive Versus Exclusive Interaction Styles in Polynesian and European Classrooms'.

7. For discussions of friendship in American culture, see, for example: Kurt Lewin, 'Some Social-Psychological Differences Between the United States and Germany', in Lewin, *Resolving Social Conflicts* (New York: Harper & Row, 1948). David Riesman, with Nathan Glazer and Reuel Denney, *The Lonely Crowd* (New Haven: Yale University Press, 1950). Philip E. Slater, *The Pursuit of Loneliness* (Boston: Beacon Press, 1970).

8. Mary Berg and Elliott A. Medrich, 'Children in Five Neighborhoods', report by the Children's Time Study, School of Law, University of California, Berkeley, 1977. Berg and Medrich, 'Children in Four Neighborhoods', *Environment and Behavior*, in press.

9. Elliott Medrich et al., *The Serious Business of Growing Up: A Study of Children's Lives Outside of School*, chap. 4 ('Children "On Their Own"'); book in preparation.

Suggested Reading

S. Holly Stocking and Diana Arezzo, *Helping Friendless Children: A Guide for Teachers and Parents*. A brief and extremely useful guidebook that shows adults how they can help teach children the skills of friendship. Available for a small charge by writing to Helping Friendless Children, Boys Town Center for the Study of Youth Development, Boys Town, Nebraska 68010.

Steven R. Asher and John M. Gottman, eds., *The Development of Children's Friendships* (New York: Cambridge University Press, in press). An excellent collection of papers, reporting recent research on various aspects of children's friendships.

William Damon, *The Social World of the Child* (San Francisco: Jossey-Bass, 1977). An integrative account of the development of children's social reasoning; addressed to a professional audience but clearly written, with many examples from children's conversations with researchers.

Hugh C. Foot, Anthony J. Chapman, and Jean R. Smith, eds., *Friendship and Childhood Relations* (London: Wiley, in press). Another good collection of research reports and reviews on children's social relationships.

Michael Lewis and Leonard A. Rosenblum, eds., *Friendship and Peer Relations* (New York: Wiley–Interscience, 1975). A valuable collection of papers on the origins of friendship. The papers focus on peer relations in the first years of life, among both humans and nonhuman primates.

Lois Barclay Murphy, *Social Behavior and Child Personality: An Exploratory Study of Some Roots of Sympathy* (New York: Columbia University Press, 1937). After forty years, this remains the richest account of children's behaviour in the pre-school setting.